SO-BWZ-293

THE TEACHING FOR SOCIAL JUSTICE SERIES

WILLIAM AYERS, SERIES EDITOR   THERESE QUINN, ASSOCIATE SERIES EDITOR

EDITORIAL BOARD: HAL ADAMS (1939–2011), BARBARA BOWMAN, LISA DELPIT, MICHELLE FINE, MAXINE GREENE (1917–2014), CAROLINE HELLER, ANNETTE HENRY, ASA HILLIARD (1933–2007), RASHID KHALIDI, KEVIN KUMASHIRO, GLORIA LADSON-BILLINGS, CHARLES PAYNE, LUIS RODRIGUEZ, JONATHAN SILIN, WILLIAM WATKINS (1946–2014)

REFUSING RACISM: WHITE ALLIES AND THE
STRUGGLE FOR CIVIL RIGHTS
  Cynthia Stokes Brown

A SCHOOL OF OUR OWN:
PARENTS, POWER, AND COMMUNITY AT
THE EAST HARLEM BLOCK SCHOOLS
  Tom Roderick

THE WHITE ARCHITECTS OF BLACK EDUCATION:
IDEOLOGY AND POWER IN AMERICA,
1865–1954
  William Watkins

THE PUBLIC ASSAULT ON AMERICA'S
CHILDREN: POVERTY, VIOLENCE, AND
JUVENILE INJUSTICE
  Valerie Polakow, Ed.

CONSTRUCTION SITES:
EXCAVATING RACE, CLASS, AND
GENDER AMONG URBAN YOUTHS
  Lois Weis & Michelle Fine, Eds.

WALKING THE COLOR LINE:
THE ART AND PRACTICE OF
ANTI-RACIST TEACHING
  Mark Perry

A SIMPLE JUSTICE:
THE CHALLENGE OF SMALL SCHOOLS
  William Ayers, Michael Klonsky, & Gabrielle H. Lyon, Eds.

TEACHING FOR SOCIAL JUSTICE:
A DEMOCRACY AND EDUCATION READER
  William Ayers, Jean Ann Hunt, & Therese Quinn

Holler If You Hear Me

ILLUSTRATED BY

XENA LOPEZ   DEON REED
CITLALI PEREZ   DALIN DOHRN
AUGUST ABITANG   ISABELLE DIZON
STEPHANY JIMENEZ TATUM HOWLETT
HENNESSY MORALES SARITA HERNÁNDEZ

COMIC EDITION

Gregory Michie
Ryan Alexander-Tanner

TEACHERS COLLEGE PRESS

TEACHERS COLLEGE | COLUMBIA UNIVERSITY

NEW YORK AND LONDON

PUBLISHED BY TEACHERS COLLEGE PRESS, 1234 AMSTERDAM AVENUE, NEW YORK, NY 10027

COPYRIGHT © 2020 BY TEACHERS COLLEGE, COLUMBIA UNIVERSITY

COVER DESIGN AND ART BY RYAN ALEXANDER-TANNER AND THE CONTRIBUTING ARTISTS

EXCERPTS FROM *THE HOUSE ON MANGO STREET*. COPYRIGHT © 1984 BY SANDRA CISNEROS. PUBLISHED BY VINTAGE BOOKS, A DIVISION OF PENGUIN RANDOM HOUSE, AND IN HARDCOVER BY ALFRED A. KNOPF IN 1994. BY PERMISSION OF SUSAN BERGHOLZ LITERARY SERVICES, NEW YORK, NY AND LAMY, NM. ALL RIGHTS RESERVED.

LYRICS FROM "FANTASY"
WORDS AND MUSIC BY MAURICE WHITE, VERDINE WHITE AND EDDIE DEL BARRIO
COPYRIGHT (C) 1977 EMI APRIL MUSIC INC. AND CRIGA MUSIC; COPYRIGHT RENEWED
ALL RIGHTS ADMINISTERED BY SONY/ATV MUSIC PUBLISHING LLC, 424 CHURCH STREET, SUITE 1200, NASHVILLE, TN 37219; INTERNATIONAL COPYRIGHT SECURED ALL RIGHTS RESERVED
REPRINTED BY PERMISSION OF HAL LEONARD LLC

ALL RIGHTS RESERVED. NO PART OF THIS PUBLICATION MAY BE REPRODUCED OR TRANSMITTED IN ANY FORM OR BY ANY MEANS, ELECTRONIC OR MECHANICAL, INCLUDING PHOTOCOPY, OR ANY INFORMATION STORAGE AND RETRIEVAL SYSTEM, WITHOUT PERMISSION FROM THE PUBLISHER. FOR REPRINT PERMISSION AND OTHER SUBSIDIARY RIGHTS REQUESTS, PLEASE CONTACT TEACHERS COLLEGE PRESS, RIGHTS DEPT.: TCPRESSRIGHTS@TC.COLUMBIA.EDU

LIBRARY OF CONGRESS CATALOGING-IN-PUBLICATION DATA IS AVAILABLE AT LOC.GOV

ISBN 978-0-8077-6325-4 (PAPER)
ISBN 978-0-8077-6326-1 (HARDCOVER)
ISBN 978-0-8077-7818-0 (EBOOK)

PRINTED ON ACID-FREE PAPER
MANUFACTURED IN THE UNITED STATES OF AMERICA

FOR ALL THE KIDS WHO HAVEN'T FELT FULLY SEEN AND HEARD IN SCHOOLS,
AND ALL THE TEACHERS WHO DO THEIR BEST TO SEE AND HEAR THEM.

CONTENTS

ACKNOWLEDGMENTS

THIS BOOK HAS BEEN A COLLABORATIVE EFFORT EVERY STEP OF THE WAY. FROM CONCEPTION TO FUNDRAISING TO RECRUITING ARTISTS TO ADAPTING THE ORIGINAL TEXT TO ILLUSTRATING TO COVER DESIGN TO PRODUCTION, IT HAS BEEN A TRULY COLLECTIVE ENDEAVOR.

OUR THANKS TO GENE BOOTH, WHO FIRST ENVISIONED *HOLLER* IN COMICS FORM YEARS AGO AND KEPT THE IDEA BOUNCING AROUND LONG ENOUGH TO SEE IT COME TO FRUITION. CAROLE SALTZ, THANKS FOR THE GREEN LIGHT.

BILL AYERS AND JOHN AYERS CHAMPIONED THIS IDEA, BELIEVED WE COULD RAISE THE MONEY TO GET IT DONE, AND TOOK CARE OF THE BIG PICTURE WHILE RYAN AND GREG WERE CONSUMED BY THE DETAILS. THIS BOOK LITERALLY WOULD NOT HAVE HAPPENED WITHOUT THEM.

WE WERE ABLE TO CONNECT WITH THE BRILLIANT YOUNG ARTISTS WHO ILLUSTRATED THIS BOOK THANKS TO THE RECOMMENDATIONS OF SEVERAL CHICAGO EDUCATORS: GLORIA TALAMANTES, HALLIE TRAUGER, JESSICA ROSENBAUM, DAN ESTEP, THERESE QUINN, GABRIELLE LYON, AND JENI CRONE. BIG THANKS TO YOU ALL!

FOR FINANCIAL ASSISTANCE TO COMPLETE THE PROJECT, WE ARE GRATEFUL FOR THE GENEROUS ASSISTANCE OF THE CROSSROADS FUND AND ILLINOIS HUMANITIES.

THE PEACE AND EDUCATION COALITION IN BACK OF THE YARDS WAS ANOTHER ESSENTIAL PARTNER. THANK YOU FOR JOINING US IN THIS ENDEAVOR AND FOR ALL YOU DO FOR THE YOUTH OF THE COMMUNITY.

THE INITIAL FUNDING TO PAY THE ARTISTS CAME FROM A GOFUNDME CAMPAIGN, AND WE'D LIKE TO THANK THE 102 GOOD PEOPLE WHO HEARD THE CALL AND GAVE US THE NEEDED ENERGY TO LIFT OFF. A SPECIAL SHOUT-OUT TO OUR YOUNGEST DONOR, J. T. BONNER, WHO, WHEN HE HEARD ABOUT THE PROJECT, INSISTED ON DONATING FIVE DOLLARS OF HIS OWN MONEY.

MANY THANKS TO OUR INITIAL EDITOR, WHITNEY TAYLOR, WHOSE KEEN EYE AND SMART SUGGESTIONS HELPED MAKE THE BOOK BETTER.

FOR HELPFUL INSIGHT AND THOUGHTFUL PROBLEM-SOLVING ON A FEW SECTIONS OF THE BOOK, THANKS TO KIM PARKER, RASHIDA QUINN, JESS THOLMER, JOSE VILSON, AND CARLA WOJCZUK.

OUR APPRECIATION TO THE FOLKS AT TEACHERS COLLEGE PRESS--BRIAN ELLERBECK, RACHEL BANKS, DAVE STRAUSS, AND KARL NYBERG--WHO SOMEHOW MANAGED TO NAVIGATE THE CRAZINESS OF A BOOK PROJECT WITH SO MANY MOVING PARTS.

ON A PERSONAL NOTE, RYAN WOULD LIKE TO THANK THE PEOPLE WHO GAVE HIM A ROOF TO SLEEP BENEATH DURING THE BOOK'S REWRITES: BILL (AGAIN) AND BERNARDINE DOHRN, CAROLE (AGAIN) AND STEVE SCHARF, ALYSSA OSWALD AND GRANDMA ROWENA. AND MOST OF ALL TO DIANA, FOR PROVIDING A FOREVER HOME.

GREG'S LOVE AND THANKS GO TO LISA, FOR THE GENTLE REMINDERS TO PUT THE SKETCHES AND THOUGHT BALLOONS ASIDE LONG ENOUGH TO MARVEL AT THE NATURAL WONDERS OF THE CITY.

THIS BOOK HAS A DUAL HEARTBEAT: ONE COMES FROM THE YOUNG PEOPLE WHO SHARED PARTS OF THEIR STORIES IN THE ORIGINAL EDITION OF *HOLLER* TWENTY YEARS AGO. THE OTHER COMES FROM THE YOUNG (AND YOUNGISH) ILLUSTRATORS WHO REIMAGINED THESE NARRATIVES IN 2019. OUR DEEPEST GRATITUDE TO YOU ALL.

AUTHORS' NOTE

WHEN GREG WROTE THE ORIGINAL EDITION OF *HOLLER IF YOU HEAR ME* IN 1999, HE HOPED IT WOULD COUNTER POPULAR MISREPRESENTATIONS OF LATINX AND BLACK YOUTH. STILL, AS A WHITE TEACHER WRITING ABOUT STUDENTS OF COLOR, HE UNDERSTOOD THAT SOME READERS MIGHT BE SKEPTICAL OF HIS MOTIVATIONS--AND FOR GOOD REASON. IN BOTH LITERARY AND NONFICTION TRADITIONS, THE TRAIL OF WHITE AUTHORS GETTING IT WRONG WHEN ATTEMPTING TO DEPICT PEOPLE AND COMMUNITIES OF COLOR IS LONG AND UGLY.

LIKE GREG, RYAN--WHO HELMED THIS TRANSFORMATION OF *HOLLER* INTO A GRAPHIC MEMOIR--IS A WHITE CIS MALE. AND LIKE THE STUDENTS FEATURED IN *HOLLER*, MANY OF THE ILLUSTRATORS OF THIS COMIC EDITION ARE YOUNG PEOPLE OF COLOR. THIS WAS INTENTIONAL: FROM THE BEGINNING, WE SOUGHT OUT CHICAGO-BASED YOUTH OF COLOR TO ADAPT THESE STORIES BECAUSE WE THOUGHT THEY WOULD BRING ADDITIONAL LAYERS OF UNDERSTANDING AND NUANCE TO THEIR INTERPRETATIONS. AND THEY DID. THEIR EXPERIENCES, VOICES, AND AESTHETICS WERE VITAL TO THE BOOK'S EVOLUTION.

THE #OWNVOICES MOVEMENT HAS REMINDED US (AT LEAST THOSE OF US WHO NEEDED A REMINDER) OF THE CRUCIAL IMPORTANCE OF SELF-REPRESENTATION FOR PEOPLE OF COLOR IN LITERATURE AND THE ARTS. THE FACT THAT WE--THE TWO PEOPLE DIRECTING THIS PROJECT-- ARE BOTH WHITE CIS MEN WASN'T (AND ISN'T) LOST ON US, AND WE UNDERSTAND THAT SOME READERS MAY FIND IT PROBLEMATIC. THIS NOTE IS NOT AN EFFORT TO ESCAPE OR DODGE THESE COMPLICATIONS AND CONTRADICTIONS--IT'S SIMPLY AN ACKNOWLEDGMENT THAT THEY EXIST, AND THAT THEY WILL, AND SHOULD, BE PART OF THE CONVERSATION ABOUT THE STORIES THIS BOOK TELLS, AND HOW IT TELLS THEM.

INTRODUCTION

SOMETIMES IT'S HARD TO BELIEVE NEARLY 30 YEARS HAVE GONE BY SINCE I FIRST STARTED TEACHING IN CHICAGO.

The Codices

IN 1999, I WROTE A BOOK ABOUT THOSE EARLY YEARS IN THE CLASSROOM CALLED *HOLLER IF YOU HEAR ME*.

HOLLER IF YOU HEAR ME

GREGORY MICHIE

MY HOPE WITH THE BOOK WAS TO COUNTER THE "WHITE HERO" NARRATIVE THAT IS SO OFTEN TOLD ABOUT CITY SCHOOLS.

WE LOVE YOU, WHITE TEACHER!!!

MY OWN TEACHING STORY WAS MORE NUANCED, MORE MESSY, MORE COMPLEX. I WASN'T TURNING KIDS' LIVES AROUND OVERNIGHT.

BUT *HOLLER IF YOU HEAR ME* ISN'T ONLY A MEMOIR OF MY EDUCATION AS A TEACHER. IT'S ALSO A VENUE FOR SOME OF MY FORMER STUDENTS TO TELL THEIR OWN STORIES.

FOR THIS 20TH ANNIVERSARY EDITION, I DECIDED TO REVISIT THE STORIES THROUGH A NEW LENS.

I REACHED OUT TO CHICAGO TEACHERS AND COMMUNITY ARTS FOLKS TO FIND TEN YOUNG ARTISTS TO ADAPT THE MATERIAL--ONE ARTIST FOR EACH OF THE BOOK'S CHAPTERS.

I ALSO ENLISTED CARTOONIST AND TEACHER RYAN ALEXANDER-TANNER TO HELP GUIDE THE PROCESS.

HEY.

I WORKED WITH THE ARTISTS TO HELP THEM EMBRACE THEIR OWN IDEAS AND AESTHETICS AND ILLUSTRATE THE STORIES AS THEY SAW THEM.

I THINK THAT WHEN WE INTRODUCE MOSES GREEN, WE SHOULD SEE A BIG, CLEAR SHOT OF HIM, TO SHOW HE'S IMPORTANT.

OH... I THOUGHT IT'D BE MORE SUSPENSEFUL IF WE SAW HIM FROM BEHIND... AND HE'S, LIKE, "MOSES," SO IT'S SUPPOSED TO LOOK LIKE HE'S "PARTING THE SEA" OF THE STUDENTS...

OH, WOW... I NEVER WOULDA THOUGHT OF THAT...

YEAH, THAT'S WAY BETTER.

IT MIGHT SEEM THAT STORIES OF A TEACHER AND HIS STUDENTS FROM THE 1990S WOULD HAVE LITTLE TO SAY ABOUT CLASSROOMS AND SCHOOLS TODAY.

BUT I FIND MYSELF STILL ASKING MANY OF THE SAME QUESTIONS I DID BACK THEN:

HOW CAN I MAKE LEARNING MORE MEANINGFUL?

HOW CAN I CREATE SPACE FOR STUDENTS' VOICES AND CONCERNS?

HOW CAN I MAKE CONNECTIONS TO THE WORLD OUTSIDE OUR CLASSROOM?

HOLLER IF YOU HEAR ME DOCUMENTS MY EARLIEST EFFORTS TO LIVE OUT ANSWERS TO QUESTIONS LIKE THESE. IT ALSO INTRODUCES YOU TO A NUMBER OF MY STUDENTS FROM THOSE YEARS, WHO REFLECT ON THEIR EXPERIENCES INSIDE AND OUTSIDE SCHOOL IN THEIR OWN WORDS.

BUT THE BOOK ISN'T JUST ABOUT THEM. IT'S ABOUT STUDENTS LIKE THEM IN CLASSROOMS AND SCHOOLS ACROSS THIS COUNTRY. MOST OF ALL, IT'S ABOUT WHAT WE OWE THEM: OUR BEST COLLECTIVE EFFORTS, AND AN EDUCATION WORTHY OF THEIR PROMISE.

ROOM TO LEARN

ILLUSTRATED BY DEON REED

I GET IT. I HAVE ONE MYSELF. BUT WHAT I WANT TO KNOW IS HOW THE WORD "BILL" RELATES TO HOW LAWS ARE MADE.

TAVARES LOVED TO DISTRACT ME FROM MY PLANNED ACTIVITIES.

OOH! MR. MICHIE! YOU KNOW WHAT MS. TUCKER DID TODAY?

DOES THIS HAVE ANYTHING TO DO WITH WHAT WE'RE TALKING ABOUT?

YEAH, SHE GOT A HUSBAND NAMED BILL.

YOU KNOW HOW WE CAN'T EAT OR DRINK OR NOTHIN' IN CLASS? WELL, TODAY SHE WAS EATIN' A DOUGHNUT AND DRINKIN' A POP RIGHT IN FRONT OF US.

NOW, THAT AINT RIGHT, MR. MICHIE. YOU KNOW THAT AINT RIGHT.

LOOK, I'M TRYING TO HELP YOU GET READY FOR THIS CONSTITUTION TEST...

BUT Y'ALL AINT FAIR! Y'ALL CAN DRINK WHENEVER Y'ALL WANT. WE GOTTA BE UP IN HERE ALL SWEATIN' AND HOT.

VINCENT! WHAT ARE YOU DOING?

I THOUGHT I HEARD SOMEBODY OUTSIDE CALLIN' ME.

IT WAS BILL!

GET BACK IN YOUR SEAT, VINCENT!

SOMETIMES IT SEEMED LIKE MY WHOLE FIRST YEAR IN THE CLASSROOM HAD BEEN ONE LONG FIGHT FOR CONTROL.

YOU'VE GOT 5 SECONDS TO GET BACK IN YOUR SEAT!

IN MANY WAYS, I WAS UNPREPARED TO BE STANDING IN FRONT OF THAT CLASSROOM.

I GREW UP IN A MIDDLE-CLASS FAMILY IN CHARLOTTE, NORTH CAROLINA. I COLLECTED BASEBALL CARDS, MEMORIZED PARTRIDGE FAMILY LYRICS, AND PLAYED NEIGHBORHOOD GAMES OF KICK THE CAN.

NC

GIANTS

REDS

IT WAS, TO A DEGREE, TYPICAL WHITE-BREAD AMERICANA.

BUT THERE WERE DIFFERENCES. BECAUSE OF WHITE FLIGHT DUE TO SCHOOL DESEGREGATION, MY NEIGHBORHOOD BECAME INTEGRATED ALMOST OVERNIGHT.

I WALKED TO SCHOOL AND PLAYED BALL WITH AS MANY BLACKS AS WHITES. BECAUSE OF THESE EARLY EXPERIENCES, I CONSIDERED MYSELF SOMEWHAT WELL-INFORMED ON ISSUES OF RACE AND CLASS. MORE, AT LEAST, THAN THE AVERAGE WHITE PERSON.

THEN I CAME TO CHICAGO.

WHILE IT WAS ONE OF THE NATION'S MOST CULTURALLY DIVERSE CITIES, IT WAS ALSO ARGUABLY THE MOST SEGREGATED. MANY OF ITS PUBLIC SCHOOLS WERE ESSENTIALLY SINGLE-RACE INSTITUTIONS.

I BEGAN SUBBING AT RALPH ELLISON IN 1990. MY FIRST DAY I WAS ASSIGNED TO A GROUP OF 8TH GRADERS WHO BARELY NOTICED ME.

THEY CALMED DOWN ONLY WHEN I OFFHANDEDLY MENTIONED THAT I'D GONE TO COLLEGE WITH MICHAEL JORDAN.

FOR REAL, YOU KNOW JORDAN!?

WELL, NOT PERSONALLY...

YOU GOT HIS NUMBER?

HE KNOW JORDAN! I CAN'T BELIEVE IT!

APPARENTLY, GETTING SUBS TO COME TO ELLISON WASN'T EASY. I THOUGHT I DROPPED THE BALL THAT DAY BUT THE PRINCIPAL INVITED ME BACK. SOON I WAS A FAMILIAR FACE.

IN NOVEMBER, THE READING LAB TEACHER ABRUPTLY RESIGNED. SHE'D TAUGHT AT A LOCAL CATHOLIC SCHOOL FOR YEARS BEFORE DECIDING SHE NEEDED A FRESH CHALLENGE.

IT WAS THE FIRST TIME I'D SEEN SOMEONE'S WILL TOTALLY BROKEN BY THEIR EXPERIENCES WITH CHILDREN. IT WOULDN'T BE THE LAST.

THE PRINCIPAL OFFERED ME THE READING LAB. SINCE MANY OF THE KIDS WERE "BELOW GRADE LEVEL" IN READING, THE LAB WAS INTENDED AS A PLACE FOR REMEDIATION.

I DIDN'T KNOW THE FIRST THING ABOUT TEACHING READING. I COULDN'T EVEN BEGIN TO PIECE TOGETHER HOW THE PROCESS WORKED.

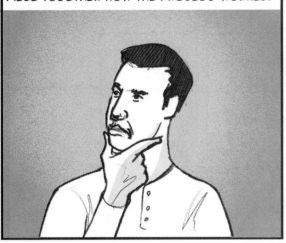

THE PRINCIPAL ALLOWED ME ONE DAY TO PREPARE. I ARRIVED EARLY TO RUMMAGE THROUGH THE LAB'S AVAILABLE RESOURCES.

THESE ARE RELICS! LOOKS LIKE I'LL HAVE TO RELY ON INSTINCTS...

THE NEXT DAY I HAD MY STUDENTS COMPLETE A QUESTIONNAIRE THAT COVERED A WIDE RANGE OF HOME-, COMMUNITY-, AND SCHOOL-RELATED TOPICS.

What kinds of things do you most enjoy reading?

What's the best book you've ever read?

I DECIDED THAT MY INITIAL GOAL WOULD BE TO SPARK THE KIDS' INTEREST IN READING USING AS MANY OUTSIDE SOURCES AS POSSIBLE.

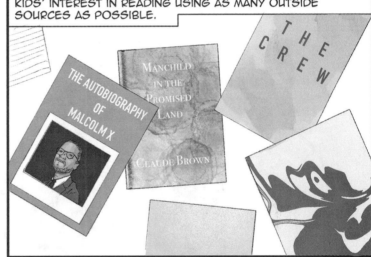

USING READINGS THAT CONNECTED TO THEIR INTERESTS AND EXPERIENCES, I MANAGED TO CREATE MOMENTS OF GENUINE ENGAGEMENT. OCCASIONALLY, LESSONS WENT WELL...

SO WHAT DO YOU THINK THIS VERSE IS SAYING?

THAT PEOPLE SELLIN' DOPE HURTIN' THEY COMMUNITY.

THE REST OF THE TIME I WAS STRUGGLING FOR SURVIVAL. I FOUND THE KIDS TO BE BRIGHT AND ENERGETIC; THEY SEEMED TO LIKE ME. BUT I OFTEN FOUND IT IMPOSSIBLE TO MAINTAIN CONTROL.

I NEVER BROKE DOWN IN FRONT OF THE STUDENTS, THOUGH I OFTEN CAME CLOSE. I KNEW IT WOULD MAKE ME APPEAR WEAKER IN THEIR EYES.

WHAT HAPPENED TO YOUR HAND, MR. MICHIE?

OH, I CUT IT WASHING DISHES.

WASHING DISHES? AINT YOU GOT A WOMAN TO DO THAT?

THIS LED TO A PERIOD-LONG DISCUSSION OF GENDER ROLES AND RELATIONSHIPS. FEW OF THE GUYS BUDGED IN THEIR POSITIONS.

WASHING DISHES...

RAYNARD, ONE OF THE GROUP'S NATURAL LEADERS, LINGERED AFTER CLASS.

YOU GOTTA BE MEANER, MR. MICHIE.

THAT'S WHAT THESE KIDS UNDERSTAND.

I'D ENCOURAGED THE KIDS TO SPEAK UP ABOUT MATTERS THAT CONCERNED THEM. I WOULD'VE PREFERRED WE TACKLE A LARGER ISSUE LIKE RACIAL DISCRIMINATION OR POLICE BRUTALITY. BUT FOR THE KIDS, THE BOTTOM LINE WAS THE SAME: UNFAIR TREATMENT.

AFTER A FEW DAYS OF DISCUSSING ROLES AND PROCEDURE, WE WERE READY FOR OUR DAY IN COURT.

NATHAN, WHO WAS ELECTED BY CLASSMATES TO SERVE AS THE PROSECUTOR, GOT THE PROCEEDINGS STARTED.

I HEARD THAT SOME TEACHERS BE EATING AND DRINKING IN THE CLASSROOM. IS THAT TRUE?

YEP.

WELL, WHAT DO YOU FEEL ABOUT THAT?

I THINK THEY SHOULD LET THE KIDS BRING IT, TOO.

THANK YOU, SIR.

TAVARES, AFTER LOSING THE CLASS VOTE, TOOK ON THE ROLE OF THE DEFENSE ATTORNEY REPRESENTING THE SCHOOL.

IS IT TRUE THAT EVERY DAY IN THE LUNCHROOM, YOU EAT THE SCHOOL FOOD?

YEAH.

THEN WHY SHOULD THE STUDENTS BE ALLOWED TO BRING CANDY AND STUFF WHEN YOU EAT THE FOOD?

'CAUSE... WELL, NOT FOOD BUT WE SHOULD BE ABLE TO BRING POP.

DO YOU EAT THE FOOD IN THE LUNCHROOM?

THE ONLY THING I EAT IS THE NUGGETS AND THE PIZZA

I THINK WE SHOULD BE ABLE TO BRING FOOD IF WE WANT. WHAT DO YOU

OBJECTION!

THE LAWYER IS NOT ON THE STAND HERE.

TAVARES RECOGNIZED THAT NATHAN WAS MAKING ARGUMENTS AND LEADING THE WITNESS. HE TOOK OVER THE QUESTIONING A FEW MINUTES LATER.

HAVE YOU EVER BROUGHT POPS IN THE SCHOOL?

YES.

EVEN THOUGH YOU WERE NOT SUPPOSED TO, BUT YOU DID?

YES.

NO FURTHER QUESTIONS, YOUR HONOR.

TAVARES WAS RAISING TO THE OCCASION. NEXT IN LINE FOR NATHAN WAS TIANNA JOHNSON.

DON'T IT BE HOT IN THOSE CLASSROOMS?

YES. IT BE SO HOT MS. SANDERS MAKE ME STAND IN THE CORNER, 'CAUSE I FALL ASLEEP.

SO DON'T YOU THINK WE SHOULD HAVE SOME POPS IN THERE?

YES, 'CAUSE IT BE TOO HOT IN THOSE CLASSROOMS.

TAVARES KNEW TIANNA WOULD BE A TOUGH WITNESS...

THINKING BACK ON MY FIRST YEAR IN THE CLASSROOM, THE TRIAL WAS THE ONE EVENT I COULD POINT TO AND SAY, "THAT'S HOW I THINK SCHOOL SHOULD BE."

I WAS MOSTLY A FACILITATOR--PROVIDING INFORMATION, HELPING ORGANIZE, KEEPING THINGS ON TRACK. BUT THE KIDS WERE THE REAL DECISION-MAKERS.

BEFORE THE TRIAL, MY STRUGGLES TO MAINTAIN CONTROL HAD LED ME TO CLASSIFY DAYS AS GOOD OR BAD BASED SOLELY ON HOW QUIET AND OBEDIENT THE CLASS HAD BEEN.

BUT THE POSITIVE ENERGY THAT SPARKED THE TRIAL REMINDED ME THAT IT DOESN'T HAVE TO BE THAT WAY. IT IS POSSIBLE--EVEN DESIRABLE--TO STEP ASIDE AND LET THE KIDS TAKE CONTROL.

SOMETIMES THAT'S WHAT BEING A TEACHER IS: KNOWING WHEN TO GET OUT OF THE WAY AND GIVE KIDS ROOM TO LEARN.

TAVARES

MY MOM, SHE WAS VERY STRICT.

SHE DROPPED OUT WHEN SHE WAS A SOPHOMORE IN HIGH SCHOOL, SO MAYBE THAT HAD SOMETHING TO DO WITH HER BEING SO STRICT ON MY SISTER AND ME.

I NEVER GOT TO DO A LOT OF THINGS THAT KIDS THAT AGE GET TO DO, LIKE GO OUTSIDE, OR GO TO THE MALL, SO WHEN I DID FINALLY GET THE CHANCE TO GET OUT, I WOULD ALWAYS BE RAMBUNCTIOUS ABOUT IT.

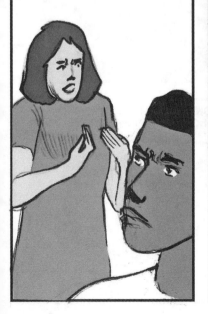

I STAYED WITH MY MOM UNTIL THE END OF MY FIRST SEMESTER AS A FRESHMAN. AFTER THAT, I MOVED IN WITH MY AUNT BECAUSE ME AND MY MOM WAS HAVING SOME PROBLEMS.

MY AUNT'S SON, WHO WAS 22--HE WAS INTO A LOT OF THINGS. SEEING HIM WITH ALL HIS MONEY, AND DIFFERENT GIRLS, THAT KINDA LURED ME SLOWLY BUT SURELY.

I GOT INVOLVED WITH A GANG, MAINLY 'CAUSE I WANTED TO MAKE SOME MONEY. SO I STARTED SELLING DRUGS AROUND WHERE I WAS STAYING.

I DIDN'T WANT TO BE LIKE SCARFACE OR ANYBODY, SO I JUST KEPT IT TO A QUARTER-OUNCE AT A TIME. I TRIED TO KEEP MYSELF ON A SHIFT. I'D GO OUT AT MAYBE 3:30 PM AND WOULDN'T COME IN 'TIL 7 AM. THAT'S A HELL OF A SHIFT.

WHEN YOU GET INVOLVED IN SOMETHING LIKE SELLING DRUGS, YOU CAN'T HAVE A CONSCIENCE. YOU CAN'T BE SOFT. SOFT PEOPLE DON'T LAST. YOU HAVE TO HAVE A, "I DON'T CARE" ATTITUDE, AND AT THAT TIME, I DIDN'T. BECAUSE ALL I SAW WAS THAT I DIDN'T HAVE NOBODY.

A PERSON THAT GANGBANGS--HE KNOWS IT'S WRONG. BUT ALL PEOPLE SEE IS THE OUTER PART. THEY NEVER LOOK WITHIN HIM TO SEE WHAT'S MAKIN' HIM DO WHAT HE DOES.

IF A PERSON WAS TO SINCERELY LOOK WITHIN THESE GUYS, THEY WOULD FIND A LOT OF SCARED YOUNG PEOPLE. SCARED OF BEING BROKE. SCARED OF NOT HAVING. SCARED OF NOT BEING ABLE TO DO FOR THEIR PARENTS OR THEIR KIDS.

AT THE END OF MY SOPHOMORE YEAR, I JUST STOPPED GOING TO SCHOOL, MAN. I HATED SCHOOL ANYWAY. I ALWAYS HATED IT.

IT'S LIKE THIS--LET'S SAY YOU DON'T KNOW HOW TO DRIVE A CAR. I CAN SAY, "WELL, YOU'RE GONNA HAVE TO PRESS DOWN ON THE BRAKE, AND THROW IT IN DRIVE..."

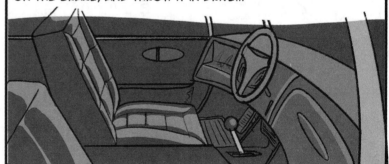

AFTER A WHILE, I CAN'T DO TOO MUCH MORE TALKING. YOU'RE GONNA HAVE TO GET BEHIND THE WHEEL AND DO IT YOURSELF. AND I THINK THAT'S HOW SCHOOL SHOULD BE. INSTEAD OF BEING TOLD HOW TO DO THINGS, YOU HAVE TO DO IT MORE YOURSELF.

I MEAN, AFTER YOU TELL ME THE BASICS--SHUT UP--LET ME DO IT NOW. THAT'S JUST HOW I AM.

BY THE TIME I QUIT SCHOOL, I DEVELOPED A "I DON'T CARE" ATTITUDE. BUT I STILL HAD MY PRINCIPLES. I WOULDN'T DO SOMETHING LIKE ROB SOMEBODY, BUT I DID GET INVOLVED IN SOME CRAZY STUFF.

ONE DAY ME AND MY COUSIN WENT OVER TO THIS GUY'S HOUSE TO COLLECT SOME MONEY AND THE GUY STARTED TALKING CRAZY. SO MY COUSIN HIT HIM.

SO THE GUY'S STILL TALKING CRAZY AND HE COMES BACK WITH A GUN. I START RUNNING AND THEN I HEAR A GUNSHOT AND I HIT THE GROUND.

MY LEG WILL NEVER BE THE SAME. I GET SHARP PAINS IN MY FOOT TO THIS DAY.

I REALIZE NOW THAT IF YOU LIVE BY THE SWORD, YOU DIE BY THE SWORD. AT THAT TIME, I WAS LIVING BY THE SWORD.

I DIDN'T CARRY A GUN. I STILL DON'T OWN A GUN TO THIS DAY. THAT'S WHY THERE'S SO MANY PEOPLE GETTING KILLED, BECAUSE THERE'S SO MANY GUNS OUT THERE.

IF THE GOVERNMENT REALLY WANTED TO MINIMIZE GUNS AND DRUGS, I THINK THEY COULD. I'M NOT SAYING THEY COULD STOP IT ALL, BUT I THINK THEY COULD CONTROL IT A LOT BETTER THAN IT IS.

ANYWAY, SOON AFTER I GOT SHOT, I WAS TOTALLY HOMELESS.

ONE DAY I WAS WALKING DOWNTOWN, MINDING MY OWN BUSINESS, AND THERE'S THIS GUY PASSING OUT FLYERS ABOUT A JOB SELLING MAGAZINES.

THE NEXT THING I KNOW I'M IN A VAN ON MY WAY TO INDIANAPOLIS, INDIANA.

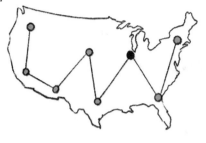

FOR THE NEXT 2 YEARS, I WAS TRAVELING AROUND THE COUNTRY, SELLING MAGAZINES. I KNOCKED ON 150 DOORS A DAY, 6 DAYS A WEEK.

AND ONE THING I LEARNED IS PEOPLE DON'T WANT MAGAZINES. AND EVEN IF THEY DO, YOU DEFINITELY DON'T HAVE TO COME TO THEIR HOUSE TO SELL THEM TO 'EM.

BUT I LEARNED A LOT IN THAT JOB. I'VE CHANGED A LOT.

RIGHT NOW I'M SCARED BECAUSE I DON'T HAVE THE EDUCATION I WANT OR NEED. I KNOW IT'S GONNA HAPPEN IN DUE TIME, BUT IT'S GETTING TO THAT POINT THAT'S THE HARD PART.

YOU KNOW, A LOT OF THE KIDS WHO SELL DRUGS, A LOT OF THEM WANNA DO RIGHT. A LOT OF THEM WANT TO BE DOCTORS AND LAWYERS.

BUT THE PROBLEM IS YOU HAVE TO STRUGGLE SO LONG TO GET TO THAT POINT, AND NOBODY WANTS TO BE BROKE.

SO A LOT OF 'EM SAY, "THIS IS WHAT I'M GONNA DO. I'M GONNA SELL DRUGS UNTIL I GET ENOUGH MONEY. THEN I CAN START DOING SOME OF THE THINGS I WANNA DO."

BUT THEY GET SO CAUGHT UP IN IT. THEY GOT REASONS FOR WHY THEY SHOULDN'T DO THESE THINGS. BUT THE REASONS FOR WHY THEY SHOULD OUTWEIGH THE REASONS FOR WHY THEY SHOULDN'T.

I WAS BLESSED WITH A GREAT MIND, AND IT'S GETTING SHARPER ALL THE TIME. SOMEDAY, AT SOME POINT IN MY LIFE, GOOD THINGS ARE GONNA HAPPEN FOR ME. I JUST GOTTA GET TO THAT POINT.

MY BIG FEAR IS, HOW LONG CAN I KEEP THE FAITH? HOW LONG CAN I CONTINUE TO BUMP MY HEAD UP THE WALL AND STILL COME OUT SWINGING? THAT'S WHAT SCARES ME.

NEVER ⬛TOUCH A⬛ STUDENT

FIVE DAYS BEFORE SCHOOL WAS SET TO OPEN FOR MY SECOND YEAR, THE FRONT PAGE REPORTED THE NEWS I'D FEARED ALL SUMMER.

CHICAGO TRIBUNE
Board of Education to Close Nine Schools

I WOULD HAVE TO GO OUT AND POUND THE PAVEMENT IN SEARCH OF A NEW JOB.

AFTER SEVERAL DISCOURAGING SCHOOL VISITS, I ARRIVED AT JOSIAH QUINCY ELEMENTARY.

96% OF THE STUDENTS WERE OF MEXICAN DESCENT, MOSTLY FIRST OR SECOND GENERATION.

JOSIAH QUINCY

ALL OF MY EXPERIENCE HAS BEEN WITH BLACK KIDS. I DON'T KNOW ANYTHING ABOUT MEXICAN IMMIGRANTS.

I CAN'T SPEAK SPANISH... I'M NOT EVEN FAMILIAR WITH THIS NEIGHBORHOOD...

I MULLED OVER MY VARIOUS INADEQUACIES AS THE PRINCIPAL EMERGED FROM HER OFFICE TO TAKE ME ON A TOUR OF THE SCHOOL.

WELCOME TO QUINCY. I'M MS. WEISMAN.

ILLUSTRATED BY TATUM HOWLETT

WE'RE EXTREMELY OVERCROWDED. THE SCHOOL WAS BUILT FOR 800 STUDENTS. WE'RE UP TO ALMOST 1,500 NOW, PRE-K THROUGH 8TH GRADE.

I ONLY HAVE ONE POSITION OPEN, AND THAT'S FOR A PULLOUT TEACHER.

QUIET!

"PULLOUT TEACHER"..?

YOU'D BE TEACHING READING AND WRITING TO SMALL GROUPS. SIX OR EIGHT KIDS AT A TIME.

THIS WOULD BE YOUR CLASSROOM. A CONVERTED COAT CLOSET.

UH... WHAT AGES WOULD I BE TEACHING?

ONE GROUP OF 2ND GRADERS. THE REST WOULD BE PULLED FROM MS. FERGUSON'S 6TH GRADE CLASS.

I'M GOING TO BE HONEST WITH YOU. SHE HAS SOME CHALLENGING STUDENTS. THEY'LL NEED A LOT OF HELP.

IF YOU'VE GOT A BETTER OFFER, I UNDERSTAND...

SEE YOU TOMORROW MORNING.

22

A FEW WEEKS LATER...

OK, WE'LL FINISH UP THE POEM TOMORROW...

LET'S TAKE A FEW MINUTES TO TALK ABOUT OUR UPCOMING TRIP TO CAMP GLENVIEW. WHAT DO YOU WANT TO DO THERE?

THANKS FOR RAISING YOUR HAND, HECTOR.

I WANT TO DO EVERYTHING THEY GOT! BUT WHAT I WANT TO DO MOST IS STAY UP LATE AND TELL SCARY STORIES.

I DON'T KNOW. THAT MIGHT GIVE SOME PEOPLE NIGHTMARES.

AY, PESADILLAS.

NOT ME! I AINT SCARED OF NOTHIN'!

ON THE MORNING OF THE CAMPING TRIP, I DROVE PAST A STRETCH OF FACTORIES AND TRUCKING YARDS AS QUINCY'S NEIGHBORHOOD CAME INTO VIEW.

ITS STREETS WERE LINED WITH AGING WOODEN TWO-FLATS AND THREE-FLATS, ORIGINALLY BUILT AS "WORKERS' COTTAGES" FOR LABORERS IN CHICAGO'S UNION STOCKYARDS, A MASSIVE LIVESTOCK-SLAUGHTERING AND MEAT-PACKING OPERATION.

"BACK OF THE YARDS" BECAME THE NEIGHBORHOOD'S NAME DUE TO ITS UNENVIABLE POSITION DOWNWIND OF THE STOCKYARD'S STENCH.

THE COMMUNITY HAD LONG BEEN HOME TO RECENTLY ARRIVED IMMIGRANTS WHO CAME TO WORK IN THE SLAUGHTERHOUSES. FIRST IRISH AND GERMAN, THEN LITHUANIANS, SLAVS, AND POLES. BY 1990, QUINCY'S QUADRANT OF THE NEIGHBORHOOD WAS ALMOST EXCLUSIVELY MEXICAN-AMERICAN.

24

I KNEW VERY LITTLE ABOUT DIANA. SHE WAS INSECURE. A POOR READER. WITHDRAWN. BUT WHAT COULD HAVE POSSIBLY PROMPTED HER TO SAY THOSE THINGS?

HAD I IGNORED HER? EMBARRASSED HER? WHAT HAD I DONE?

DURING MY FIRST YEAR AS A TEACHER, I HEARD A LOT OF ADVICE FROM VETERAN TEACHERS:

DON'T GIVE THE KIDS TOO MUCH FREEDOM.

YOU CAN'T BE THEIR FRIEND.

BUT THE WORDS REPEATED MORE OFTEN THAN ANY OTHERS WERE:

NEVER TOUCH A STUDENT!

PRINCIPAL WEISMANN

IT'S LIKELY A RESPONSE TO THE NUMEROUS HIGH-PROFILE LAWSUITS FILED AGAINST TEACHERS ACCUSED OF EITHER STRIKING OR FONDLING THEIR STUDENTS.

I WAS DEFINITELY AGAINST PUNITIVE OR ILL-MOTIVATED PHYSICAL CONTACT, BUT I ALSO BELIEVED THAT A BIG PART OF TEACHING WAS SHOWING KIDS YOU CARE FOR THEM, WHICH IS HARD TO DO WHEN YOU ALWAYS KEEP THEM AT ARM'S LENGTH.

Knock Knock

PRINC
WEISM

MY MIND WAS RACING. THERE WAS NO WAY I COULD GO TO CAMP NOW. I TOLD MS. WEISMAN THE WHOLE STORY WITHOUT WAITING FOR A REACTION.

LET'S BACK UP A BIT. HAS DIANA SAID ANYTHING TO YOU IN CLASS? HAVE THEIR BEEN ANY COMMENTS?

NO. NOTHING.

HAVE YOU EVER TOUCHED HER? EVEN IN A FRIENDLY WAY? A PAT ON THE BACK? ANYTHING?

I DID A THOROUGH SEARCH OF MY MENTAL FILES...

NO. NOT ONCE. I'M SURE.

OK, MR. MICHIE. I KNOW YOU'RE FEELING BADLY RIGHT NOW, BUT I THINK YOU SHOULD GO AHEAD AND GO TO CAMP.

I'LL GET DIANA DOWN HERE THIS MORNING AND FIND OUT WHAT'S HAPPENING WITH HER. CALL ME TONIGHT AND I'LL TELL YOU WHAT I FOUND OUT.

CAMP GLENVIEW RESEMBLED AN INGENIOUSLY WELL-SCRIPTED PARODY OF THE CAMPING EXPERIENCE.

YET, AS SHODDY AND UNINSPIRED AS IT SEEMED TO ME, MY STUDENTS LIKELY SAW IT MUCH DIFFERENTLY. WHEN THE ONLY OPEN SPACES YOU SEE ARE PARKING LOTS, A SIMPLE PATCH OF WOODS CAN BE AN ASTOUNDINGLY LIBERATING EXPERIENCE.

THAT EVENING, I CALLED MS. WEISMAN...

EVERYTHING'S FINE.

APPARENTLY, DIANA HAD WANTED TO ATTEND CAMP, BUT HER FATHER REFUSED TO BUY HER SOME NECESSARY SUPPLIES, SAYING HE DIDN'T HAVE THE MONEY. TOO EMBARRASSED TO EXPLAIN THIS TO THE OTHER KIDS, SHE RESORTED TO FICTION.

DIANA SAID SHE SINGLED ME OUT BECAUSE SHE DIDN'T LIKE ME AND DIDN'T FEEL COMFORTABLE AROUND ME.

AGAIN, I RACKED MY BRAIN TO THINK OF WHAT I MIGHT'VE DONE TO MAKE HER FEEL THIS WAY.

BUT MORE THAN THAT, I WORRIED ABOUT THE REVERSE SCENARIO: I WONDERED IF I WOULD EVER BE ABLE TO FEEL COMFORTABLE AROUND DIANA AGAIN.

WOULD I BE ABLE TO PUT ALL THIS ASIDE, TO FORGIVE AND FORGET? COULD I TREAT HER FAIRLY? COULD I BE HER TEACHER?

AFTERWARDS, I STOPPED IN AT ONE OF THE BOYS' CABINS FOR THEIR NIGHTLY BED CHECK.

THIS GUY STARTED IT!

I AINT START NOTHIN'!

YOU MESS WITH MY COVERS AGAIN, I'LL MESS WITH YOUR FACE!

ALL RIGHT, HECTOR, LET'S GO.

NO!

HECTOR, I NEED TO TALK WITH YOU ABOUT THIS OUTSIDE. RIGHT NOW.

HE BETTER NOT MESS WITH MY COVERS WHILE I'M GONE, NEITHER.

WHAT WAS ALL THAT ABOUT?

HECTOR? I'M TALKING TO YOU...

I THOUGHT YOU WERE LOOKING FORWARD TO THIS.

WE'RE HERE TO MAKE NEW FRIENDS, REMEMBER? NOT ENEMIES.

sniff

WHAT'S WRONG? WHY ARE YOU CRYING?

MY SISTER'S SICK.

SINCE WHEN?

TONIGHT SHE STARTED FEELING SICK... HER COUNSELOR TOOK HER TO SEE THE DOCTOR...

I SUDDENLY REMEMBERED THAT THIS PERSON SITTING NEXT TO ME WAS A CHILD. I HAD BECOME SO CAUGHT UP IN THE FRONT HE MAINTAINED I FORGOT THERE WAS A REAL PERSON UNDER THERE.

I'M SCARED...

I WANTED TO COMFORT HIM, TO LET HIM KNOW HE WASN'T ALONE, BUT THE FAMILIAR WORDS OF CAUTION CAME CREEPING IN: NEVER TOUCH A STUDENT.

I CHASED THE WORDS FROM MY MIND.

I UNDERSTAND HOW YOU FEEL.

IT'S SCARY WHEN SOMEONE YOU CARE ABOUT IS SICK. I THINK SHE'LL BE OK.

CAN WE GO SEE HER?

WE CAN TRY.

I THOUGHT AGAIN OF DIANA ROJAS, AND HOW I HAD NEVER REALLY TRIED TO SEE HER UNTIL THAT MORNING.

UNTIL THEN, SHE HAD NEVER DEMANDED MUCH OF MY ATTENTION, SO SHE HAD NEVER GOTTEN MUCH OF IT.

I HAD BEEN BUSY HELPING OTHER KIDS, AND HER LIGHT HAD GOTTEN LOST IN THE HOLLOW GLOW OF MY GOOD INTENTIONS. I WONDERED IF I'D EVER SEE IT NOW.

IT'S NICE OUT HERE, AINT IT?

YEAH, IT IS.

HECTOR

AFTER SPENDING TIME IN AN ALTERNATIVE SCHOOL AND A SHORT-TERM PSYCHIATRIC CARE FACILITY, HECTOR LEFT SCHOOL FOR GOOD A MONTH INTO HIS FRESHMAN YEAR. HE IS 17.

I HATED SCHOOL, BUT I HAD NO CHOICE. I HAD TO GO 'CAUSE MY MOM WOULD LOCK THE DOOR AND THROW ME OUT.

I HATED MATH THE MOST BECAUSE I DIDN'T KNOW HOW TO DO IT. BUT I DIDN'T WANT THE OTHER KIDS TO KNOW, SO I JUST DIDN'T TRY. I JUST ACTED LIKE I DIDN'T CARE.

ACTING ALL BAD BUT I DIDN'T KNOW HOW TO DO MATH.

I REMEMBER SOME OF THE STUFF WE DID. LIKE THAT MAGIC BOX YOU BROUGHT IN, WHERE WE HAD TO IMAGINE WHAT WAS INSIDE.

AND WHEN I GOT THAT AWARD IN YOUR CLASS, THAT MICHIE AWARD THAT YOU PUT IN PLASTIC AND EVERYTHING. THAT WAS SO COOL 'CAUSE IT MADE ME FEEL LIKE I WAS DOING SOMETHING GOOD.

ONE TIME, I WAS COMING DOWN THE STAIRS, AND I DIDN'T LIKE THE WAY THIS ONE TEACHER WAS LOOKING AT ME.

WHAT YOU LOOKIN' AT? WHAT, DO I OWE YOU SOMETHING?

DON'T YOU EVER TALK TO ME LIKE THAT AGAIN!

SLAM

THIS LADY'S CRAZY!

THEN THE NEXT DAY SHE GOES AND TELLS THE PRINCIPAL AND I GET IN TROUBLE.

IF I WOULD'VE BEEN DOING WHAT I WAS SUPPOSED TO DO, THEN THAT WOULDN'T HAVE HAPPENED. I JUST WISH THE TEACHERS WOULD'VE CONCENTRATED ON ME MORE, SPENT MORE TIME WITH ME. BUT I KNOW THEY COULDN'T.

TEACHERS WOULD TELL ME...

YOU'RE GONNA GET KICKED OUT OF HERE. THIS SCHOOL DOESN'T NEED YOU.

I GOT IN THE GANG FOR RESPECT. THAT WAS THE MAIN THING.

I'D SEE THEIR CARS, THEIR MONEY, THEY'D BE CRUISING AROUND, PUMPING THEIR SOUNDS, AND I LIKED IT.

BUT WHEN I REALLY LOOK AT IT, THEY TREATED ME KINDA LOW. THEY'D GET ME HIGH AND TAKE ME CRUISING, BUT WHEN I GOT PUT AWAY, I SAW WHO MY REAL FRIENDS WERE. NONE OF 'EM CAME TO SEE ME, MAN. NOT ONE.

I DON'T THINK PRISON REALLY HELPS PEOPLE. IT JUST MAKES THEM CRAZIER. INSTEAD OF PUTTING THEM IN JAIL, THEY SHOULD TAKE ALL THE GANGBANGERS AND PUT THEM IN THE ARMY. THAT'S WHAT I'D DO.

WHAT AFFECTED ME MOST GROWING UP WAS MY ENVIRONMENT.

I WONDER WHY WE DON'T GOT A YMCA OR A YOUTH CLUB OR A BOYS' CLUB BY OUR NEIGHBORHOOD. SOME NEIGHBORHOODS HAVE ALL THAT STUFF.

MY FATHER WAS NEVER AROUND. IF HE WOULD'VE BEEN THERE, THINGS WOULD'VE BEEN DIFFERENT. BUT HE AINT HERE.

SO I JUST GOTTA MOVE ON. I GOTTA SEE LIFE DIFFERENT, DO SOMETHING WITH MYSELF.

I KNOW THERE'S MAGIC IN A BOX SOMEWHERE. I JUST GOTTA FIND IT. I WANNA LEAVE THE NEIGHBORHOOD, GO TO THE MARINES. I NEED TO GO FAR AWAY. REAL, REAL FAR AWAY.

I NEED TO GET AWAY FROM THIS ENVIRONMENT FOR A LONG, LONG TIME. SOMEPLACE DIFFERENT. SOMEPLACE WHERE I CAN GO AND FISH FOR THE REST OF MY LIFE.

TERRIBLE HORRIBLE NO GOOD VERY BAD!

ALEXANDER HAD A TERRIBLE, HORRIBLE, NO GOOD, VERY BAD DAY. WE ALL DO SOMETIMES. CAN YOU REMEMBER HAVING A DAY LIKE THAT?

JESSE?

I RODE THE BUS WITH MY ABUELO AND IT BROKE DOWN. WE HAD TO WAIT AND IT WAS RAINING.

ANOTHER BUS CAME AND IT SPLASHED US AND KEPT DRIVING. ABUELO SAID BAD WORDS IN SPANISH!

VERONICA?

I HAD SOME BIRDS AND, UM, ONE DAY THE MOM KILLED THE DAD BIRD AND, UM, WE HAD TO THROW THE DAD AWAY.

MR. MICHIE, HAVE YOU EVER HAD A TERRIBLE, HORRIBLE, NO GOOD, VERY BAD DAY?

WELL, I—

RING!

ILLUSTRATED BY XENA LOPEZ

AT THE END OF THE DAY, I HAD AN AFTER-SCHOOL ENRICHMENT PROGRAM WITH MS. FERGUSON'S 6TH GRADE CLASS.

THESE STUDENTS WERE OFTEN REFERRED TO AS "THE LOW GROUP."

I'D HEARD ONE TEACHER CALL THEM, "STUPID" AND ANOTHER LABEL THEM, "THE CRIMINALS," BASED ON TWO OF THE BOYS HAVING POLICE RECORDS.

THE SCHOOL ADMINISTRATION HAD DECIDED TO SEPARATE THEM ALL INTO ONE GROUP. THESE 26 STUDENTS AND I FINISHED OUT EACH SCHOOL DAY TOGETHER.

JUST DO WHAT YOU CAN WITH THEM.

THE KIDS WERE WELL AWARE OF HOW THEY WERE PERCEIVED BY SOME OF THE ADULTS IN THE BUILDING.

OUR WHOLE CLASS IS DUMB.

YOU'RE NOT DUMB, ARMANDO.

EVEN THE THINGS YOU DO THAT YOU'RE NOT SUPPOSED TO DO TAKE BRAINS. YOU HAVE TO BE SMART TO FOOL THE TEACHER.

YEAH, BUT WE'RE STILL STUPID. WHY DO YOU THINK THEY PUT US ALL IN THIS CLASS?

THAT'S NOT—

SOMETHING LIKE THIS SHOULD NEVER HAPPEN. NOT IN A CLASSROOM WHERE PEOPLE RESPECT AND TRUST EACH OTHER. I'M TRYING—

REMEMBER
☆ BE NICE
☆ CONSIDER CHO
☆ ALWAYS SP

THAT'S IT FOR YOU. I'VE ASKED YOU TWICE ALREADY. WE'RE GOING TO SEE MR. MANNING AFTER SCHOOL.

I DON'T CARE, YOU DUMBO!

...LOOK, I'M TRYING TO HELP YOU GUYS, BUT I NEED YOUR HELP, TOO.

I WANT YOU TO PARTICIPATE IN THIS, BUT YOU CAN'T BE SHOOTING RUBBER BANDS AND CALLING PEOPLE NAMES. IS THAT ASKING TOO MUCH?

...NO.

HA HA HA

CAN YOU HELP ME OR NOT?

HA HA HA HA HA HA HA

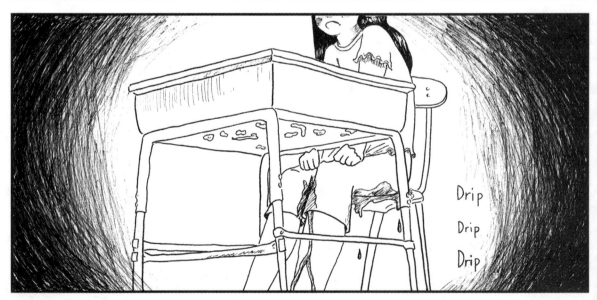

45

TERRIBLE.

HORRIBLE.

NO GOOD.

VERY BAD.

IT WAS TEMPTING TO LAY ALL OF THE BLAME ON THE KIDS. AFTER ALL, I WAS TRYING MY BEST TO HELP THEM. WHY DID THEY HAVE TO RESIST? WHY COULDN'T THEY RESPOND THE WAY I WANTED THEM TO?

BUT IT WASN'T THEIR FAULT. AT LEAST, NOT ALL OF IT.

THESE KIDS KNEW THE DEAL. AT BEST, THE SCHOOL WAS TREATING THEM AS LESS THAN ADEQUATE. AT WORST, THEY WERE BEING DEMONIZED.

SHOULD ANYONE HAVE BEEN SURPRISED WHEN THEY ACTED SO AGGRESSIVELY RESENTFUL?

IN THE DAYS AND WEEKS THAT FOLLOWED, THE SESSIONS REMAINED DIFFICULT. MY PRIMARY GOAL WAS TO HELP THE KIDS VIEW THEMSELVES AS SMART, TALENTED, AND CAPABLE INDIVIDUALS.

MY SUCCESS, THOUGH, WAS MEAGER. YEARS OF LOW EXPECTATIONS AND MARGINALIZATION WOULD TAKE MORE THAN 10 WEEKS TO REMEDY.

GREAT POEM, ARMANDO.

THANKS.

I WISH YOU COULD BE OUR TEACHER NEXT YEAR.

MAYBE I CAN.

DON'T PICK ME.

NO?

NO, I MEAN, I WANT TO BE IN YOUR CLASS...

I JUST DON'T WANNA BE DUMB NEXT YEAR.

ARMANDO

NOW A HIGH SCHOOL JUNIOR, AGE-WISE, HE IS STILL A FIRST-SEMESTER FRESHMAN BY HIS CREDENTIALS.

IN 6TH GRADE, I HAD MS. FERGUSON. SHE WAS A GOOD TEACHER, BUT OUR CLASS, WE GOT LEFT OUT.

THEY SEPERATED US FROM THE OTHER KIDS.

I THOUGHT THE OTHER CLASSES WERE SMARTER THAN US. PEOPLE USED TO CALL US "THE TROUBLE-MAKERS," SO I USED TO WALK THE HALLS THINKING I WAS ALL BAD. I FELT LIKE EVERYBODY WAS SCARED OF ME, AND THAT'S HOW I WANTED IT.

BUT NOW, WHEN I THINK ABOUT HOW I WAS BACK THEN, I THINK, "WHAT A GOOF. WHAT AN IDIOT."

LAST YEAR, I HAD A GOOD ENGLISH TEACHER. IT WAS INTERESTING IN THERE. WE DID PROJECTS AND MADE POSTERS FOR BOOKS WE READ.

BUT I WAS ABSENT A LOT.

MY ENGLISH TEACHER WOULD CALL MY MA ALL THE TIME, 'CAUSE SOMETIMES I'D SKIP HER CLASS.

IT KIND OF MADE ME MAD, BUT I GUESS SHE CARED ABOUT ME. THE PROBLEM'S NOT THE TEACHERS. THE PROBLEM IS ME.

I KNOW THE TEACHERS ARE TEACHING GOOD 'CAUSE I SEE OTHER SUDENTS WITH GOLD ID'S. I'M JUST WALKING AROUND WITH A PLAIN GREEN ONE.

IT'S IMPORTANT TO ME TO GRADUATE, 'CAUSE I WANT A JOB THAT PAYS BETTER. MY DAD'S A LANDSCAPER.

I DON'T WANT YOU TO WORK LIKE ME, LIKE A RABBIT.

MY MOM, SHE ALWAYS TELLS ME SHE WANTS ME TO FINISH. SOME DAYS WHEN I DON'T FEEL LIKE GOING, SHE TELLS ME

ARMANDO, YOU'RE GONNA GO TO SCHOOL.

IF YOU WANT ME TO GO SO BAD, HOW COME YOU DIDN'T GO?

I SHOULDN'T HAVE SAID THAT.

'CAUSE SHE REALLY COULDN'T FINISH SCHOOL. SHE WAS THE OLDEST IN HER FAMILY IN MEXICO, AND SHE HAD TO HELP OUT MY GRANDMA AND GRANDFATHER. THEY HAD A LITTLE STORE. SHE WENT UP TO 6TH GRADE, I THINK. MY DAD WENT TO 3RD.

I DON'T GO OUT THAT MUCH ANYMORE, 'CAUSE OF WHAT HAPPENED LAST WINTER.

I CAME TO MY STOP AND GOT OFF, AND THEY FOLLOWED ME.

WHAT YOU BE ABOUT?

I'M NOT NOTHING, MAN. I KNOW YOU, CHUCHO. WE USED TO GO TO SCHOOL TOGETHER.

YOU DON'T KNOW ME. MY NAME AINT CHUCHO!

I THOUGHT I WAS GONNA DIE, BUT THEN THEY JUST RAN OFF.

AND THEN IN SCHOOL...

WHAT ARE YOU DOING COMING IN HERE LATE?

NOT OVER THERE! SIT OVER HERE, NOW!

A FEW MINUTES LATER, THIS OTHER TEACHER CAME IN

...what

YOU CAN'T BE SITTING THERE BLOCKING THE DOORWAY LIKE A SLOB!

I DIDN'T SAY ANYTHING. I DIDN'T WANT TO GET IN TROUBLE, SO I JUST STAYED QUIET, 'CAUSE THE TEACHER'S GONNA WIN ANYWAY.

THE TEACHER'S ALWAYS GOTTA WIN.

IN THE PARENT CONFERENCES, THE TEACHER'LL COME UP WITH ALL KINDS OF BAD STUFF FROM A LONG TIME AGO.

HE NEVER GOES TO SCHOOL. HE CUTS CLASS. HE DON'T DO HIS HOMEWORK. HE DON'T PAY ATTENTION.

AND I FEEL LIKE, "WHY DON'T YOU TELL HER ABOUT THE GOOD THINGS I DO? I'M NOT ALL BAD."

IF TEACHERS WANT KIDS TO DO BETTER, WHY DO THEY SUSPEND THEM? THEY SHOULD BE KEEPING THEM IN SCHOOL, NOT KICKING THEM OUT.

SOMETIMES YOU FEEL LIKE THEY DON'T EVEN WANT YOU THERE.

THE STORY OF THEIR LIVES

IN THE SPRING OF 1991, I PICKED UP *THE HOUSE ON MANGO STREET* BY SANDRA CISNEROS AT A BOOK STORE NEAR THE UNIVERSITY OF CHICAGO.

AS CLICHE AS IT SOUNDS, I WAS IMMEDIATELY DRAWN TO IT, AND COULDN'T PUT IT DOWN.

I READ THE FIRST HALF OF THE BOOK RIGHT THERE IN THE AISLE AND FINISHED IT THAT NIGHT. THE STORY STAYED WITH ME FOR DAYS.

THE BOOK CENTERS ON ESPERANZA CORDERO, A YOUNG MEXICAN-AMERICAN GIRL GROWING UP IN A WORKING-CLASS BARRIO.

AROUND THE SAME TIME, ONE OF MY GRAD SCHOOL PROFESSORS WAS CONSTANTLY ENCOURAGING ME TO BRING MY STUDENTS' LIVES AND EXPERIENCES INTO THE CURRICULUM.

BUT SINCE I'D COME TO QUINCY, THAT HAD BECOME HARDER FOR ME TO DO.

ILLUSTRATED BY ISABELLE DIZON

AT ELLISON, I WAS ABLE TO INCORPORATE AFRICAN-AMERICAN CULTURE...

...HOWEVER, QUINCY WAS ANOTHER WORLD. I KNEW NOTHING ABOUT THE EXPERIENCES OF MEXICAN-AMERICANS.

BUT THIS BOOK...

ESPERANZA'S EXPERIENCES MIRRORED THOSE OF MANY OF THE KIDS AT QUINCY. IT WAS THE PERFECT BOOK TO USE WITH MY 6TH GRADE STUDENTS.

BUT WHEN WE TRIED READING IT, IT WAS SLOW GOING. THE KIDS LOVED THE STORIES, BUT BECAUSE OF THEIR READING DIFFICULTIES, CISNEROS' POETIC LANGUAGE AND RICH NARRATIVE WERE OFTEN LOST.

I HAD AN IDEA:

WHAT IF I ENLISTED A COUPLE OF 8TH GRADE GIRLS TO BE THE VOICE OF ESPERANZA IN AN AUDIOBOOK VERSION OF *THE HOUSE ON MANGO STREET*?

I THOUGHT MY PULLOUT STUDENTS WOULD UNDERSTAND THE BOOK BETTER IF IT WAS READ TO THEM.

AND SO...

OH! HI!

ARE YOU GUYS HERE ABOUT *THE HOUSE ON MANGO STREET?*

MMM... I GUESS SO.

MR. FABIAN TOLD US YOU WERE GOING TO HAVE TRYOUTS FOR SOME KIND OF READING PROGRAM OR SOMETHING.

YOU'RE AT THE RIGHT PLACE. COME ON IN.

NONE OF THEM HAD HEARD OF THE BOOK, SO I EXPLAINED THAT, LIKE THEM, THE AUTHOR WAS MEXICAN-AMERICAN AND HAD GROWN UP IN CHICAGO.

I TOLD THEM WE WOULD MEET THE NEXT MORNING BEFORE SCHOOL AND HAVE TRYOUTS. I WOULD LISTEN TO EACH OF THEM READ.

THE GIRLS LISTENED POLITELY BUT I COULDN'T MEASURE THEIR INTEREST.

HI, MR. MICHIE.

WE WERE WONDERING...

LIKE, DO YOU THINK WE COULD ALL DO IT?

WHAT DO YOU MEAN?

WELL, MR. FABIAN TOLD US YOU WERE LOOKING FOR TWO PEOPLE TO READ, BUT--WELL, WE ALL LIKED THE STORIES AND ALL OF US WANT TO DO IT.

...I WAS REALLY ONLY PLANNING TO USE A COUPLE DIFFERENT VOICES...

BUT IF YOU ALL WANT TO BE A PART OF IT, THEN--WELL, I GUESS YOU'LL ALL BE A PART OF IT.

WE'LL JUST HAVE FIVE ESPERANZA'S.

SOON WE WERE MEETING REGULARLY...

HA HA HA HA HA HA HA HA HA HA HA HA HA HA HA

WHAT'S SO FUNNY?

THE TITLE OF THIS STORY... "CHANCLAS."

THAT'S JUST NOT THE KIND OF WORD YOU EXPECT TO SEE IN A BOOK.

IT'S NOT BAD, IS IT?

NO, NOT BAD...

IT'S JUST... I DON'T KNOW HOW TO EXPLAIN IT.

THEY'RE SHOES, RIGHT?

YEAH, LIKE THE KIND... ¿COMO SE LLAMA EN INGLES?

FLIP FLOPS. THERE YOU GO!

WHAT'S SO FUNNY ABOUT FLIP FLOPS?

IT'S JUST THE WORD, LIKE A NICKNAME OR SOMETHING.

I'VE NEVER SEEN IT PRINTED UP IN A BOOK BEFORE. IT'S NOT THAT IT'S FUNNY, IT'S JUST... LIKE AN INSIDE WORD. YOU GET ME?

THE MORE WE READ, THE CLEARER IT BECAME TO ME THAT EVERY STORY IN THE BOOK WAS FILLED WITH SUCH ELEMENTS. DETAILS AND NUANCES ONLY AN INSIDER--A MEXICAN-AMERICAN--WOULD KNOW.

WE READ BEFORE SCHOOL ONE OR TWO MORNINGS EACH WEEK.

WE DISCUSSED THE STORIES AND THE GIRLS TRIED TO EXPLAIN CULTURAL REFERENCES I DIDN'T UNDERSTAND.

THE VIGNETTES IN THE BOOK NEVER FAILED TO CONJURE UP MEMORIES FROM THE GIRLS' OWN LIVES, AND WE SPENT AS MUCH TIME SHARING THESE AS WE DID READING THE BOOK.

BY FEBRUARY OF THAT SCHOOL YEAR, THEY WERE CALLING THEMSELVES:

THE MANGO GIRLS

ALEJANDRA   YAJAIRA   MARISSA   NANCY   VERONICA

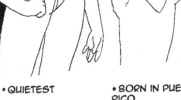

- SERIOUS BOYFRIEND (IN 8TH GRADE TERMS)
- SKILLED ARTIST

- QUIETEST
- RESPONSIBLE BABYSITTER

- BORN IN PUERTO RICO
- DREAMS TO BE A LAWYER

- INTROSPECTIVE
- WILL BE THE FIRST IN HER FAMILY TO GRADUATE COLLEGE

- QUICK-WITTED
- NATURAL PERFORMER

57

YOU LIVE RIGHT HERE, 4006 MANGO.

ALICIA SAYS, AND POINTS TO THE HOUSE I AM ASHAMED OF.

NO, THIS ISN'T MY HOUSE.

I SAY, AND SHAKE MY HEAD AS IF SHAKING COULD UNDO THE YEAR I'VE LIVED HERE. I DON'T BELONG. I DON'T EVER WANT TO COME FROM HERE.

"I DON'T EVER WANT TO COME FROM..."

UGH.

COULD I START OVER?

UH, SURE, GO AHEAD. BUT HANG ON A SECOND...

...NANCY, YOU OK?

YEAH, I'M FINE.

YOU SURE NOTHING'S WRONG?

I'M SURE.

TELL HIM.

IF IT'S SOMETHING YOU DON'T WANT TO TALK ABOUT TELL HIM!

I JUST DON'T WANT TO MAKE A BIG DEAL OF IT...

OUR HOUSE BURNED DOWN LAST NIGHT.

OH MY GOD!

IT'S OK. EVERYBODY'S ALL RIGHT. NOBODY DIED OR ANYTHING.

DID IT BURN... EVERYTHING?

YEAH. EVERYTHING'S RUINED, EITHER FROM THE FIRE OR THE SMOKE OR THE WATER.

I HAD TO BORROW CLOTHES FROM MY AUNT. MY SISTERS DON'T EVEN HAVE SHOES.

YOU DIDN'T HAVE TO COME, YOU KNOW. WE WOULD HAVE UNDERSTOOD.

I WANTED TO. I DON'T KNOW WHY. I JUST WANTED TO BE HERE...

CAN WE PLEASE JUST KEEP READING?

THAT AFTERNOON, I GAVE NANCY MY COPY OF *THE HOUSE ON MANGO STREET* TO USE OVER THE WEEKEND.

I TOLD HER I'D BUY HER A NEW ONE AND GIVE IT TO HER ON MONDAY.

REALLY, MR. MICHIE, I'D RATHER JUST KEEP THIS ONE.

PUT IT THIS WAY.

WOULD YOU RATHER HAVE AN OLD FRIEND OR A NEW FRIEND?

3-18-'92

Dear Sandra Cisneros,

We have been reading your wonderful book, The House on Mango Street. We enjoyed it ~~mostly because~~ reading the real life situations and relating them to our own lives. We are in ~~a drama~~ an eighth grade Dramatic Reading Group at Quincy Elementary School in the southwest of Chicago. We are planning to record the stories so other students can listen to them. We would like to know how much of your story is based on your life. Your stories are very exciting, funny and touching.

We would really like to meet you. If you ever get a chance to come to Chicago, you can contact our teacher, Mr. Greg ~~Miller~~ Michie at Quincy ~~Elementary~~ in Chicago, Illinois. Once again, we really enjoyed ~~the~~ your book.

WHAT DO YOU THINK?

CAN WE SEND IT TO HER?

I THINK IT'S A GREAT LETTER. WE COULD SEND IT TO HER PUBLISHER, AND MAYBE THEY'D FORWARD IT ON TO HER.

DO YOU THINK SHE'LL ANSWER?

DO YOU THINK SHE'LL COME, MR. MICHIE?

WHAT I THINK IS,

SANDRA CISNEROS IS A VERY BUSY WOMAN. SHE MIGHT NOT HAVE TIME TO WRITE YOU BACK. I HOPE SHE DOES, BUT... DON'T COUNT ON IT.

IT DOESN'T MEAN SHE DOESN'T APPRECIATE YOUR LETTER.

...SO YOU THINK WE SHOULD TAKE THAT PART OUT ABOUT COMING TO VISIT?

I JUST DON'T WANT YOU TO BE DISAPPOINTED.

I DON'T MEAN TO BE NEGATIVE. I'M JUST BEING HONEST. I THINK THE CHANCES OF HER COMING ARE, LIKE, THIS BIG.

WE COULD TAKE THAT PART OUT.

WHY? I SAY WE SHOULD LEAVE IT. YOU NEVER KNOW, THAT'S WHAT I SAY.

THAT'S TRUE. YOU NEVER KNOW.

I JUST HOPED SHE ANSWERED THEIR LETTER.

A CARD. A NOTE. ANYTHING.

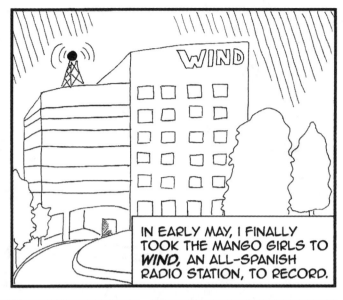

IN EARLY MAY, I FINALLY TOOK THE MANGO GIRLS TO **WIND,** AN ALL-SPANISH RADIO STATION, TO RECORD.

THEY ALL HAD JITTERS AT FIRST...

BUT THE GIRLS ROOTED FOR EACH OTHER, REVELED IN EVERY STORY, HUNG ON EVERY WORD.

BY EARLY AFTERNOON, WE HAD TAPED ALL 25 STORIES.

THOUGH THE PROJECT WAS DONE, THE GIRLS WANTED TO CONTINUE OUR MORNING MEETINGS.

WE BEGAN TO TALK ABOUT THEIR FUTURES.

ALL OF YOU CAN BE IN COLLEGE IN 4 YEARS IF THAT'S WHAT YOU WANT.

EVERY ONE OF YOU HAS WHAT IT TAKES.

BUT WHEN YOU GET THERE –

DON'T FORGET THIS:

WHEN YOU LEAVE YOU MUST REMEMBER TO COME BACK FOR THE OTHERS. A CIRCLE, UNDERSTAND?

YOU WILL ALWAYS BE ESPERANZA. YOU WILL ALWAYS BE MANGO STREET.

YOU CAN'T ERASE WHAT YOU KNOW. YOU CAN'T FORGET WHO YOU ARE.

—CLICKITY—
—CLACKITY—
—CLICKITY—
—CLACKITY—

IN CELEBRATION OF OUR TIME TOGETHER, I GOT EACH GIRL A COPY OF "NORTH OF THE RIO GRANDE," AN ANTHOLOGY OF SHORT STORIES ON THE MEXICAN-AMERICAN EXPERIENCE, AND TYPED UP FOR EACH A PAGE-LONG PROPHECY OF MY PREDICTIONS AND WISHES FOR THEIR NEXT 20 YEARS.

THE NEXT WEEK, THE MANGO GIRLS GRADUATED FROM QUINCY, OFFICIALLY MOVING INTO HIGH SCHOOL.

THEY NEVER RECEIVED A RESPONSE TO THEIR LETTER TO SANDRA CISNEROS.

EARLY IN THE FOLLOWING SCHOOLYEAR.

MR. MICHIE?

YES?

CAN YOU TAKE A PHONE CALL?

YEAH, I'LL TAKE IT IN RHONDA'S OFFICE.

THIS IS GREG.

HI. MY NAME IS SUSAN BERGHOLZ. I'M CALLING FROM NEW YORK.

I'M CALLING ON BEHALF OF SANDRA CISNEROS.

SANDRA RECIEVED A LETTER FROM A FEW OF YOUR STUDENTS LAST SPRING. SHE ASKED ME TO SEE IF WE COULD SET UP A VISIT.

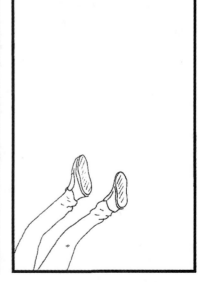

ON THE MORNING OF DECEMBER 17, THE MANGO GIRLS AND I STOOD SIDE BY SIDE IN THE AUDITORIUM WHILE A SEA OF KIDS TOOK THEIR SEATS.

THE GIRLS WERE EXCUSED FROM THEIR HIGH SCHOOLS FOR THE DAY...

TO MEET THE AUTHOR HERSELF, SANDRA CISNEROS.

AFTER MY OPENING REMARKS, EACH GIRL STEPPED TO THE MICROPHONE TO READ ONE OF HER FAVORITE SELECTIONS FROM MANGO STREET.

AND WHEN IT WAS CISNEROS'S TURN, SHE HAD THE KIDS EXPLODING IN LAUGHTER ONE MINUTE, LOST IN INTROSPECTION THE NEXT.

I'M VERY PROUD OF MY CULTURE.

SHE TOLD THEM THAT BEING MEXICAN WAS WHAT MADE HER WRITING SO SPECIAL.

AFTER THE ASSEMBLY, I WATCHED FROM THE SIDELINES AS THE GIRLS MET WITH CISNEROS IN THE LIBRARY.

THEY DIDN'T ACT LIKE THEY WERE MEETING A CELEBRITY. IT WAS MORE LIKE THEY WERE WELCOMING HOME A FRIEND.

THEY WEREN'T AWESTRUCK, JUST APPRECIATIVE AND RESPECTFUL TOWARDS SOMEONE WHO KNEW WHAT IT WAS LIKE TO BE IN THEIR CHANCLAS. SOMEONE WHO HADN'T FORGOTTEN.

N A N C Y

NANCY IS NOW A FRESHMAN AT DEPAUL UNIVERSITY--ONLY A FEW MILES AWAY ON CHICAGO'S NORTH SIDE, BUT WORLDS APART FROM THE LIFE SHE'S KNOWN. SHE IS THE FIRST OF HER MOTHER'S 9 CHILDREN TO ATTEND COLLEGE AND IS STUDYING TO BECOME A TEACHER.

I WENT TO A HISPANIC LEADERSHIP CONFERENCE AT THE END OF MY JUNIOR YEAR IN HIGH SCHOOL THAT REALLY MOTIVATED ME.

SO I GO HOME AND MY MA'S MAD, 'CAUSE I CAME HOME LATE.

LOOK, MA, I THINK I CAN GO HERE!

NANCY, WHAT ARE YOU TALKING ABOUT?

¡COLEGIO!

YOU'RE NOT GOING TO COLLEGE.

SHE SAID WE DIDN'T HAVE THE MONEY. I TOLD HER I COULD GET SCHOLARSHIPS, BUT SHE DIDN'T REALLY UNDERSTAND IT.

SHE HAS THIS IDEA THAT ONLY RICH PEOPLE GO TO COLLEGE.

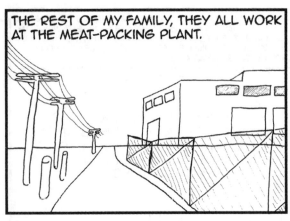

THE REST OF MY FAMILY, THEY ALL WORK AT THE MEAT-PACKING PLANT.

THEY MAKE PRETTY GOOD MONEY, BUT THEY WORK ABOUT 14 OR 16 HOURS A DAY, DOING HEAVY STUFF.

FOR MOST GIRLS IN MY NEIGHBORHOOD, GOING TO COLLEGE, THAT'S SOMETHING BEYOND

WOW! YOU'RE GOING TO *COLLEGE!*

FOR THE CAUCASIANS, GOING TO COLLEGE IS NORMAL.

THAT'S NICE, DEAR.

IF YOU DO GO TO COLLEGE, SOME OF YOUR FRIENDS WILL SAY

YOU'RE TRYING TO ACT WHITE.

MY SISTER TOLD ME THE OTHER DAY

NANCY, YOU'RE STARTING TO TALK WHITE.

IT'S LIKE, YOU CAN'T WIN.

THIS SEMESTER, I WROTE AN ESSAY ABOUT, "WHO AM I?" AND ONE OF THE THINGS I PUT WAS

AND MY TEACHER WROTE A LITTLE COMMENT

Although I was born in the United States, I consider myself Mexican. I remember my uncles would call me over and, "Nancy, aver, de de eres?" and I respo...

Nancy, you're Mexican AMERICAN

I DON'T MIND BEING CALLED MEXICAN-AMERICAN, BUT I'D RATHER SAY I'M MEXICAN.

IN THE MAJORITY OF MY CLASSES, I'M THE ONLY LATINO. EVEN THE MEXICANS THAT ARE HERE, A LOT OF THEM DIDN'T COME FROM NEIGHBOR-HOODS LIKE MINE.

AT THE BEGINNING OF THE YEAR, I WAS REAL INTIMIDATED IN MY CLASSES. I DIDN'T WANT TO SPEAK UP BECAUSE I DIDN'T FEEL LIKE WHAT I HAD TO SAY WAS AS INTELLECTUAL AS OTHER PEOPLE.

IS IT GONNA COME OUT THE WAY I WANT IT TO COME OUT?

SOMETIMES I WRITE DOWN WHAT I'M GONNA SAY FIRST, SO I DON'T MESS IT UP.

IT'S DIFFERENT LIVING UP HERE ON THE NORTH SIDE. A LOT OF TIMES I FEEL LIKE AN OUTSIDER.

ONE NIGHT, ME AND MY FRIENDS WERE GOING TO GO DOWNTOWN WITH THESE OTHER GIRLS. THEY WERE ALL WHITE. BUBBLY WHITE.

ONE TIME I WAS WAITING FOR THE TRAIN AND SOME BLACK GUY CAME UP TO ME AND TRIED TO SELL ME SOCKS!

I WAS, LIKE, SO FREAKED OUT! I DIDN'T EVER WANT TO TAKE THE TRAIN AGAIN!

THE BUBBLIEST OF ALL

OH MY GOD!

POOR YOU!

WOULD YOU LIKE A CADENA?

IF THEY WENT TO MY NEIGHBORHOOD, IT WOULDN'T JUST BE SOCKS. PEOPLE WOULD TRY TO SELL THEM ELOTES, CADENAS, T-SHIRTS... THEY'D SHIT IF THEY CAME TO MY NEIGHBORHOOD!

FRESH ELOTES!

WHEN SANDRA CISNEROS CAME TO QUINCY, IT WAS LIKE A HERO STORY FOR ME.

THE MAIN THING I REMEMBER THAT SHE SAID IS

DON'T FORGET WHERE YOU CAME FROM.

IN A POOR NEIGHBORHOOD, IT'S LIKE PEOPLE BECOME SUCCESSFUL, AND THEN YOU NEVER SEE THEM AGAIN.

I TOLD MY MA I DON'T WANT TO MOVE OUT OF HERE. I PLAN TO TEACH AT QUINCY.

I THINK IT WOULD BE NICE FOR A KID TO HAVE A TEACHER WHO CAN SAY

I LIVE RIGHT NEXT DOOR TO YOU, AND I'VE LIVED HERE ALL MY LIFE.

I THINK THE KIDS WILL LOOK AT ME DIFFERENT. THEY CAN SAY

MY TEACHER LIVES IN MY NEIGHBORHOOD.

SHE'S LIVED HERE ALL HER LIFE.

SHE'S JUST LIKE ME.

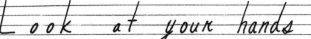

I HAD NEVER HEARD THE WORD BRAZER BEFORE I BEGAN TEACHING AT QUINCY. I BROUGHT IT UP ONE DAY TO ONE OF MY COLLEAGUES, BOB FABIAN.

I GUESS YOU COULD CALL IT ANGLICIZED SPANISH.

IT COMES FROM THE WORD BRAZO. IT MEANS ARM.

IT STARTED DURING WORLD WAR 2. ALL THESE GUYS HAD GONE OFF TO FIGHT SO THE U.S. GOVERNMENT MADE AN AGREEMENT WITH MEXICO.

MEN WERE SENT UP HERE TEMPORARILY TO PICK CROPS AND WORK ON FARMS.

TO WORK WITH THEIR ARMS. THEIR BRAZOS.

THEY CALLED IT THE BRACERO PROGRAM BUT THE WHITE GUYS--THEIR BOSSES--COULDN'T PRONOUNCE IT SO THEY JUST STARTED CALLING THEM BRAZERS.

BRAZERS

ILLUSTRATED BY SARITA HERNÁNDEZ

TO OUR STUDENTS, BRAZER MEANS SOMEONE WHO'S *TOO* MEXICAN...

...THE ONES WHO DON'T SPEAK ENGLISH, DON'T WEAR $100 GYM SHOES, AREN'T AMERICANIZED AT ALL. THEY LOOK DOWN ON THOSE KIDS.

THE KIDS' CONFUSION ABOUT THEIR ETHNIC IDENTITIES SEEMED TO STEM FROM A CLASH OF CULTURES BETWEEN THEIR SEPERATE LIVES AT HOME AND SCHOOL.

AT HOME, MOST KIDS SPOKE SPANISH...

PRIMER iMPACTO

SPEAK ENGLISH ONLY

AT SCHOOL, THERE WAS A TEACHER WHO FINED THEM WHEN THEY DIDN'T SPEAK ENGLISH.

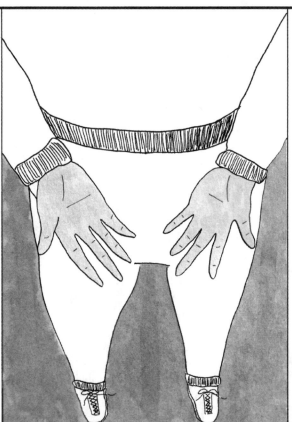

THE FACT THAT SOME OF THE KIDS VIEWED AMERICAN CULTURE AS SUPERIOR TO THEIR OWN WAS REALLY NO SURPRISE. IT WAS BEING OFFERED UP-- CONSCIOUSLY OR NOT--AS WHAT WAS NORMAL, AVERAGE, OR EVEN IDEAL.

THE UNDERLYING MESSAGE WAS THAT IF THEY WANTED TO FIT IN--AND WHAT KID DOESN'T--THEY FIRST NEEDED TO LEAVE THE WAYS OF THEIR ANCESTORS IN THE MEXICAN DUST.

FOR MY 2ND YEAR AT QUINCY, I WAS ASSIGNED TO WORK WITH 7TH AND 8TH GRADERS. ONCE AGAIN, MY CLASSROOM WAS A CONVERTED COAT CLOSET. IT WAS ADJACENT TO BOB'S CLASSROOM, AND THIS GAVE ME AN IDEA.

WHAT IF WE TAUGHT OUR CLASSES TOGETHER?

YOU MEAN, INSTEAD OF PULLING KIDS OUT, YOU'D BE IN MY CLASSROOM, TOO?

YEAH! TEAM TEACHING.

LET ME THINK ABOUT IT...

BOB AND I CONTINUED TO DISCUSS OUR HOPES FOR THE KIDS AND OUR VISIONS OF AN IDEAL CLASSROOM. WE AGREED THAT MOST KIDS WERE FRUSTRATED BY TRADITIONAL LANGUAGE ARTS CLASSES, WHERE GRAMMAR AND SPELLING WERE TAUGHT WITH NO REAL PURPOSE.

LANGUAGE ARTS • DICTIONARY • THESAURUS • VOCABULARY • PHONICS • GRAMMAR • COMPOSITION

MLA CITATION
ENGLISH
US AMERICAN LITERATURE
SHAKESPEARE   POETRY

WE BEGAN TO EXPLORE THEMES AND IDEAS THAT COULD BE MEANINGFUL TO THE KIDS.

JUSTICE • STEREOTYPES • THE MEDIA • GENDER • GANGS • GENTRIFICATION • ABILITY

HOW ABOUT STARTING WITH THEM? HOW ABOUT BEGINNING WITH A FEW WEEKS ON WHAT IT MEANS TO BE MEXICAN-AMERICAN?

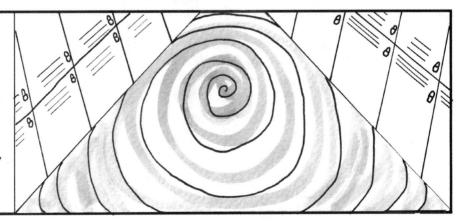

BOB AND I AGREED TO START THERE. MANY OF THE STUDENTS AT QUINCY SEEMED TO FEEL AS IF THEY WERE IN LIMBO. NOT REALLY MEXICAN, BUT NOT TRULY AMERICAN, EITHER.

THIS MEANT I HAD TO BEGIN EDUCATING MYSELF. I WENT TO THE PUBLIC LIBRARY AND CHECKED OUT A STACK OF RESOURCES.

I READ BOOKS OF POETRY AND SHORT STORIES BY MEXICAN AND MEXICAN-AMERICAN AUTHORS.

I READ BOOKS ON MEXICAN HISTORY AND MEXICAN-U.S. RELATIONS.

I STUDIED MEXICAN MYTHS AND LEGENDS AND CLIPPED NEWS ARTICLES ABOUT CURRENT DEVELOPMENTS IN THE COUNTRY.

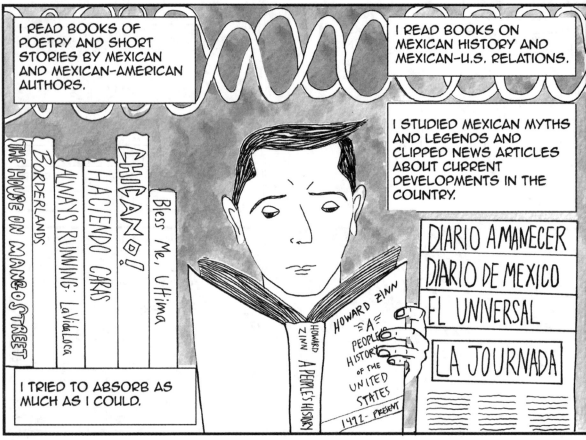

THE HOUSE ON MANGO STREET

BORDERLANDS

ALWAYS RUNNING: La Vida Loca

HACIENDO CARAS

CHICANO!

Bless Me, Ultima

HOWARD ZINN A PEOPLE'S HISTORY

HOWARD ZINN A PEOPLE'S HISTORY of the UNITED STATES 1492-PRESENT

DIARIO AMANECER

DIARIO DE MEXICO

EL UNIVERSAL

LA JOURNADA

I TRIED TO ABSORB AS MUCH AS I COULD.

MEXICAN   MEXICAN AMERICAN   AMERICAN

BOB DID BACKGROUND WORK OF HIS OWN AND WE POOLED OUR RESOURCES TO COME UP WITH A 5-WEEK SCHEDULE OF ACTIVITIES FOR OUR MEXICAN-AMERICAN UNIT.

WE BEGAN IN FAIRLY TRADITIONAL FASHION WITH A 3-DAY SERIES OF TAG-TEAM LECTURES ON THE HISTORY OF MEXICO AND MEXICANS IN THE UNITED STATES. IT ALMOST SOUNDS INSULTING NOW--3 PERIODS TO PRESENT THE ENTIRE HISTORY OF A PEOPLE--BUT WE HAD TO PUT THINGS IN SOME SORT OF HISTORICAL CONTEXT.

WE ATTEMPTED TO PRESENT THE HISTORY OF MEXICO NOT AS ONE STORY, BUT MANY, WHICH COULD BE SEEN FROM A MULTITUDE OF PERSPECTIVES;

WE READ AND DISCUSSED MEXICAN LEGENDS SUCH AS LA LLORONA...

LISTENED TO MARIACHI AND OTHER TRADITIONAL MUSIC...

COMPARED THE MURALS OF DIEGO RIVERA TO THOSE FOUND IN MEXICAN NEIGHBOR-HOODS IN CHICAGO.

A COUPLE WEEKS INTO THE UNIT, WE SCHEDULED A "SHOW AND TELL" SESSION IN WHICH STUDENTS WOULD BRING A CULTURALLY RELATED OBJECT FROM HOME AND GIVE A PRESENTATION ABOUT ITS SIGNIFICANCE TO THEM OR THEIR FAMILY.

BOB KICKED IT OFF BY PASSING AROUND SOME LEATHER BOOTS AND A SILVER RING THAT HAD THE AZTEC SUN STONE ENGRAVED ON IT.

SHOW AND TELL

AS I GET OLDER, I CONNECT MORE AND MORE TO MY MEXICAN ROOTS.

ONE BY ONE, THE KIDS FOLLOWED...

ENRIQUE BROUGHT IN A CAN OF BEER.

SOME KIDS BROUGHT PHOTOS OF GRANDPARENTS.

ONE GIRL BROUGHT IN A WOOL BLANKET THAT BELONGED TO HER AUNT.

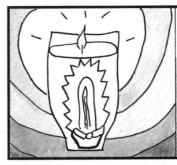

ANOTHER GIRL BROUGHT A VOTIVE CANDLE DEPICTING LA VIRGEN DE GUADALUPE, MEXICO'S PATRON SAINT.

THE INTEREST LEVEL WAS HIGH, BUT A FEW KIDS WHO WERE CALLED ON WEREN'T READY...

TOMORROW'S THE LAST CHANCE.

IF YOU COME IN UNPREPARED, YOU'RE GOING TO STAND UP IN FRONT OF THE CLASS FOR 2 MINUTES ANYWAY.

THE NEXT DAY, BOB WAS OUT SICK. AFTER TEACHING ON MY OWN ALL DAY, I WASN'T IN THE BEST MOOD WHEN SHOW-AND-TELL TIME CAME AROUND.

SERGIO, YOU'RE UP FIRST.

I DON'T GOT IT.

WELL, YOU REMEMBER WHAT I SAID. NOW YOU HAVE TO GET UP THERE ANYWAY.

COME ON, MR. MICHIE...

GO ON, GET UP THERE.

SHOW AND TE

I'M NOT SURE HOW LONG SERGIO STOOD THERE BEFORE I REALIZED HE WAS ABOUT TO CRY.

I ASKED HIM TO STEP OUT INTO THE HALL. EVENTUALLY, HE EXPLAINED THAT HIS GRANDMOTHER WAS IN THE HOSPITAL. HE'D SPENT THE PREVIOUS NIGHT ON A COUCH IN THE HOSPITAL LOBBY.

I'D ASSUMED SERGIO DIDN'T DO THE ASSIGNMENT BECAUSE HE WASN'T INTERESTED IN LEARNING ABOUT HIS CULTURE. BUT AFTER LISTENING TO HIM, I WAS REMINDED THAT CULTURE IS SOMETHING THAT IS LIVED. SERGIO CARED ABOUT HIS SCHOOLWORK, BUT HIS ABUELA CAME FIRST.

I'M SO SORRY...

SERGIO WOULDN'T TALK TO ME FOR A LONG TIME AFTER THAT. I DIDN'T BLAME HIM.

THE UNIT ENDED UP TAKING LONGER THAN WE'D PLANNED. AND THROUGHOUT IT, STUDENTS WROTE: NARRATIVES, PERSONAL ESSAYS, POETRY.

NOT ALL THE KIDS WERE EAGER TO PUT WORDS TO THE PAGE, OF COURSE.

I DON'T KNOW WHAT TO WRITE.

I CAN'T THINK OF ANYTHING.

BUT MANY WERE INSPIRED. AS A CULMINATING PROJECT, WE COLLECTED SOME OF THEIR COMPOSITIONS IN A BOOKLET.

MIS PENSAMIENTOS

QUINCY MIDDLE SCH

FOR MANY OF THEM, IT WAS THE FIRST TIME THEY HAD BEEN ABLE TO TELL THIS PART OF THEIR STORIES INSIDE OF THE SCHOOL.

JOAQUIN DURAN WAS A KID WHO HAD ONLY BEEN IN THE UNITED STATES FOR A FEW YEARS. HE WANTED TO TELL THE STORY OF ONE OF HIS ANCESTORS AS HIS GRANDFATHER HAD TOLD IT TO HIM.

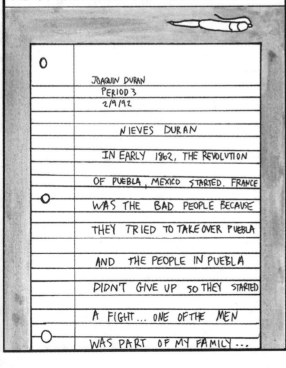

JOAQUIN DURAN
PERIOD 3
2/9/92

NIEVES DURAN

IN EARLY 1862, THE REVOLUTION
OF PUEBLA, MEXICO STARTED. FRANCE
WAS THE BAD PEOPLE BECAUSE
THEY TRIED TO TAKE OVER PUEBLA
AND THE PEOPLE IN PUEBLA
DIDN'T GIVE UP SO THEY STARTED
A FIGHT... ONE OF THE MEN
WAS PART OF MY FAMILY...

WHEN THE FRENCH GOT TO THEIR PART OF PUEBLA, THEY START TO DO BAD THINGS TO WOMEN. NIEVES DURAN MADE A TUNNEL AND PUT FOOD AND HID THEIR DAUGHTER. THE FRENCH CAME AND HE DIDN'T TELL THEM SO THEY SHOT HIM IN THE EYE...

NIEVES DURAN WAS A HERO TO JOAQUIN, BUT HE CERTAINLY WOULDN'T APPEAR IN ANY HISTORY BOOKS AT QUINCY.

PERLA CERDA WOULDN'T HAVE FOUND ANYONE LIKE HER FRIEND ROSALBA IN SCHOOLBOOKS, EITHER.

> Rosalba has been living in America for 10 months now, but she is still afraid to go anywhere because she's afraid of the migra cause they might catch her. She's been trying to convince her husband to go back to Mexico. Her life has been miserable living in an attic.

ELIZABETH WAS A STUDENT WHO WAS BORN WITH A LYRICAL GRACE. FOR HER, WORDS AND IDEAS WERE MEANT TO BE SHARED, NOT GRADED.

> mexico! we finally get there. Grandpa, grandma, tía monchix, "mexico" my real home I had imagined it different but anyways, I'm still glad to be here. I realize that even though I was born in Mexico, I was raised here in Chicago, I'm a Mexican raised here in a different country. I'm not a "prayer" like they say, not a Chicana either.

GABRIEL, IN ARGUING AGAINST ACCEPTING A STRICTLY AMERICAN IDENTITY, REVEALED THAT WHILE HIS GRASP OF THE BIG PICTURE WAS NOT YET FIRM, HE WAS AT LEAST BEGINNING TO SEE ONE.

> JUST BECAUSE I AM PARTLY AMERICAN INSIDE, I DON'T THINK I AM AMERICAN, EVEN THOUGH I WAS BORN ONE.
> FIRST, I DON'T GET TREATED WELL BY TEACHERS WHO ARE PREJUDICED, MANY TEACHERS GET MAD BECAUSE I TALK IN SPANISH IN THE ROOM.
> SECOND, I DON'T GET TREATED LIKE AN AMERICAN. THIRD, WE MEXICANS CAN'T GET THINGS LIKE GOOD LAWYERS THAT HAVE WON MANY TRIALS...

OUR ENTIRE LANGUAGE ARTS CURRICULUM THAT YEAR DEVELOPED OUT OF THE MEXICAN-AMERICAN IDENTITY THEME.

WE SPENT THE SECOND QUARTER LOOKING AT RACISM AND ITS MANIFESTATIONS, THE THIRD QUARTER EXPLORING WOMEN'S ROLES IN SOCIETY AND GENDER ISSUES, AND THE FINAL 10 WEEKS ON A STUDY OF OTHER CULTURES AND COUNTRIES.

IT WAS A DIFFERENT KIND OF LANGUAGE ARTS CLASS THAN ANY OF US HAD EXPERIENCED BEFORE.

WE REALLY DIDN'T USE BOOKS. INSTEAD USED VIDEO CAMERAS, STORIES AND KNOWLEDGE OF THE PEOPLE. WE ALSO LEARNED NO MATTER WHAT WE SHOULD HAVE RESPECT FOR EVERY PERSON.

TO BEGIN TO HAVE A TRUE RESPECT FOR MY KIDS, I HAD TO GET TO KNOW THEM NOT ONLY AS INDIVIDUALS, BUT ALSO AS PEOPLE IN A PARTICULAR CONTEXT: CHILDREN OF MEXICAN IMMIGRANTS, LIVING IN A WORKING-CLASS NEIGHBORHOOD ON THE SOUTH SIDE OF CHICAGO, WITHIN AN INCREASINGLY XENOPHOBIC LARGER SOCIETY, IN THE 1990'S.

I COULDN'T HELP KIDS HONOR AND RESPECT THEIR RICH LEGACY AS MEXICANS AND AS WORKING PEOPLE IF I ONLY DID SO IN VAGUE TERMS MYSELF. THEIR STORIES FORCED ME TO TAKE A FRESH LOOK AT HOW I FIT INTO THE BIGGER PICTURE--TO STEP BACK AND LOOK AT MY OWN HANDS. BUT IT WAS ONLY A BEGINNING. I KNEW I HAD A LOT YET TO LEARN ABOUT THE KIDS WHO CALLED ME THEIR TEACHER.

I REMEMBER ONCE WHEN I WAS IN 4TH GRADE, SOMEONE WHO HAD JUST COME FROM MEXICO GOT PUT IN OUR CLASSROOM, WHICH WAS NOT BILINGUAL.

WHY SHOULD I START TRYING TO LEARN YOUR LANGUAGE WHEN YOU'RE COMING TO MY COUNTRY?

YOU'RE IN AMERICA AND HERE WE SPEAK ENGLISH. WHY SHOULD I LEARN YOURS?

I THOUGHT AMERICA WAS SUPPOSED TO BE A PLACE WHERE ALL DIFFERENT CULTURES CAN COME AND LEARN FROM EACH OTHER.

AND NOW THEY'RE THINKING ABOUT CLOSING THE BORDER SO MEXICAN PEOPLE CAN'T COME IN. THEY'RE COMING HERE FOR THE SAME REASON WHITE PEOPLE CAME HERE.

WHY SHOULD THE DOORS GET CLOSED NOW?

I THINK ALL MEXICAN PEOPLE EXPERIENCE SOME RACISM. NO MATTER WHAT YOU DO, THERE'S GONNA BE PEOPLE OUT THERE WHO LOOK DOWN ON YOU.

OPEN

NO DOGS NO MEXICANS

MY FATHER IS REAL SUPPORTIVE OF ME. HE ASKS ME WHAT I WANT TO DO, AND THEN TRIES TO HELP ME WITH WHATEVER I NEED.

BUT SOMETIMES I THINK HE WANTS SO MUCH FOR ME TO SUCCEED THAT HE GOES OVERBOARD AND PRESSURES ME.

I GO TO SCHOOL ALL DAY...

THEN I GO TO WORK FOR HIM UNTIL 8...

THEN COME HOME AND DO MY HOMEWORK AND THEN I STILL HAVE TO PRACTICE MY SINGING.

SOMETIMES I JUST WANT TO EXPLODE, I JUST WANT TO DO SOMETHING ELSE.

MY FATHER TOLD ME ONCE THAT I WAS THE HOPE FOR BRINGING THE FAMILY UP, TO BE THE FIRST ONE TO GRADUATE FROM COLLEGE. SO THAT'S WHAT I WANT TO DO.

I'VE NEVER LIKED HISTORY OR SOCIAL STUDIES. THE WAY THEY TEACH IT IS--IT'S A HISTORY BOOK. YOU OPEN IT, AND IT SAYS COLUMBUS DID THIS, COLUMBUS DID THAT--AND I THINK IT'S ANOTHER EXAMPLE OF THE WHITE MAN'S THINKING ABOUT WHAT WENT ON, FROM THEIR POINT OF VIEW. WHY DON'T WE HEAR THE INDIAN'S SIDE?

WHEN YOUR CULTURE IS BROUGHT INTO A CLASS AT SCHOOL, IT MAKES YOU FEEL GOOD BECAUSE YOU KNOW THAT YOUR CULTURE ISN'T JUST BEING RECOGNIZED FOR, "OH, TODAY THEY CAUGHT 5 IMMIGRANTS CROSSING THE BORDER" OR WHATEVER.

I ASKED MY FATHER WHAT WERE SOME OF THE TRADITIONS HE LOST COMING OVER HERE. I STARTED TO REALIZE THAT THAT'S PART OF THE PRICE OF COMING HERE--YOU LOSE PART OF YOUR CULTURE.

I CONSIDER MYSELF MEXICAN. I GREW UP IN THE UNITED STATES, I WAS BORN HERE, I PRETTY MUCH LIVE THE LIFE OF AN AMERICAN. BUT I DON'T CARE.

MEXICAN IS WHAT I AM. IT'S IN MY BLOOD. AND I DON'T THINK I'LL EVER LOSE THAT. IT'S VERY IMPORTANT TO ME TO HOLD ONTO IT.

NO ZOMBIES ALLOWED

I BEGAN MY 4TH YEAR AS A TEACHER IN MY OWN FULL-SIZED CLASSROOM, AT THE HELM OF A NEW COURSE I'D PROPOSED.

THIS CLASS IS CALLED MEDIA STUDIES.

I WANT TO BE CLEAR THAT THE POINT OF THIS CLASS IS NOT TO TURN YOU INTO MOVIE STARS,

OR EVEN TO TEACH YOU HOW TO OPERATE A VIDEO CAMERA.

IT'S TO HELP YOU BE MORE CONFIDENT IN EXPRESSING YOURSELF.

AND TO HELP YOU REALIZE THAT EACH OF YOU HAS IMPORTANT THINGS TO SAY.

IT'S ABOUT TEACHING YOU TO LOOK AT TELEVISION AND OTHER MEDIA MORE CRITICALLY.

ANY QUESTIONS?

WHEN DO WE GET TO USE THE CAMERAS?

ILLUSTRATED BY HENNESSY MORALES

SO MUCH FOR MY STRATEGICALLY PLANNED INTRODUCTION...

TEACHING YOU TO MAKE MEDIA WITHOUT TEACHING YOU TO UNDERSTAND IT SEEMS LIKE A BAD IDEA.

THIS COURSE IS DESIGNED TO COMBINE THE BASICS OF PRODUCTION WITH A CRITICAL STUDY OF MASS MEDIA.

WE'RE GOING TO USE VIDEO AS A WAY FOR YOU TO EXPRESS YOUR CREATIVITY AND IDEAS.

FACTS

BUT WE'RE ALSO GOING TO LEARN TO QUESTION, ANALYZE, AND EVALUATE THE MESSAGES YOU GET FROM THE MEDIA.

WHAT ARE YOU HIDING?

WHEN WE TURN ON THE TV, WE CAN'T TURN OFF OUR BRAINS.

HEY, MAYBE...

YEAH, YEAH. IN A SEC.

TO SUCCEED IN THIS CLASS, YOU HAVE TO THINK...

NO ZOMBIES ALLOWED

SORRY, NOT ON THE LIST.

NOW LET'S BEGIN.

SHUT UP! Y'ALL DON'T KNOW ME!

JERRY Springer

I'M A 13-YEAR-OLD PROSTITUTE

ALRIGHT, THAT'S ENOUGH.

C'MON, MR. MICHIE.

HER MOM'S GONNA COME OUT AND THEY'RE GONNA BOX!

IT'S SO PREDICTABLE. IF YOU'VE SEEN ONE OF THIS GENRE,* YOU'VE SEEN THEM ALL...

*VOCAB WORD: GENRE

WHAT'S CONSISTENT ABOUT THE REPRESENTATION OF YOUNG PEOPLE WE'VE SEEN IN TALK SHOWS?

...

ALRIGHT, LET'S SAY YOU'RE FROM ANOTHER PLANET. YOU DON'T KNOW ANYTHING ABOUT HUMANS...

WHAT'S UP?

...AND YOUR SPACESHIP LANDS AT THE JERRY SPRINGER SHOW.

WHAT ARE YOU GOING TO THINK THAT TEENAGERS ARE LIKE?

CRAZY.

DANGEROUS.

DISRESPECTFUL.

IT'S A LOT OF STEREO-TYPES.*

*VOCAB WORD: STEREOTYPE

GOOD! NOW LET'S DECONSTRUCT* WHAT WE JUST SAW...

THE MORE YOU KNOW

*VOCAB WORD: DECONSTRUCT

WE'D ALREADY AGREED THAT THE #1 AIM OF ANY COMMERCIAL TV PROGRAM WAS TO TURN A PROFIT.

WHAT DO YOU THINK THE SHOW'S PURPOSE IS BESIDES MAKING MONEY?

I THINK IT WAS TO HELP THE GIRL TO STOP USING DRUGS AND BEING A PROSTITUTE.

THEY WEREN'T TRYING TO HELP HER!

GIVE HER A CHANCE, CLAUDIO.

SILVIA, WHY DO YOU THINK THAT?

WELL, AFTER SHE TOLD ABOUT ALL THE STUFF THAT SHE DONE, JERRY ASKED IF SHE WANTED TO STOP...

AND THEN THE AUDIENCE ALL STARTED CHEERING LIKE SHE COULD JUST STOP 'CAUSE HE SAID SO. THAT'S STUPID!

I DON'T THINK THEY HAD ANY RESPECT FOR THE GIRL. UNDERNEATH HER NAME THEY PUT, "13-YEAR-OLD PROSTITUTE" LIKE THAT WAS HER JOB.

SHE WAS JUST UP THERE MAKING A FOOL OF HERSELF 'CAUSE SHE WANTED TO BE ON TV.

DO YOU THINK THE GIRL GOT USED IN A SENSE BY THE PRODUCERS AND THE HOST?

YEAH.

AND WE GET USED, TOO. 'CAUSE WE WATCH 'EM.

AFTER A SERIES OF DISCUSSIONS ABOUT REPRESENTATION IN MEDIA, I INVITED MY STUDENTS TO WRITE A LETTER TO THE NETWORK OF THEIR CHOICE.

FOX, I REALLY LIKE YOUR NETWORK. BUT I HAVE ONE PROBLEM.

YOU HAVE A STEREOTYPE ABOUT LATINOS. AND THAT STEREOTYPE IS NEGATIVE.

FOR EXAMPLE, IN "COPS" THE LATINOS AND BLACKS ARE ALMOST ALL THE TIME THE BAD PEOPLE. AND THE WHITE PEOPLE ARE THE COPS.

ALSO, EVERY TIME WE WATCH YOUR COMEDY SHOWS, WE NEVER SEE MEXICANS OR ARABIANS AS THE MAIN CHARACTERS.

THE MAIN REASON THIS BOTHERS ME SO MUCH IS NO ONE REALLY KNOWS WHAT THE MEXICAN AND ARABIAN CULTURES ARE ALL ABOUT BECAUSE THEY'RE ALWAYS SHOWN AS THE BAD GUYS OR MADE FUN OF.

101 WAYS TO UPSET PEOPLE

I'M NOT SAYING YOU'RE THE ONLY NETWORK THAT DOES THAT BUT YOU'RE ONE OF THE MAIN NETWORKS AND MAYBE YOU CAN CHANGE A FEW THINGS.

I WOULD APPRECIATE IT IF YOU CAN ANSWER MY LETTER. THANK YOU.

COMING SOON

The Aventures of BUTTERFLY and MOTH

Only on FOX

WE NEVER RECEIVED ANY RESPONSE FROM FOX.

SINCE MEDIA STUDIES HAD NO TEXTBOOK OR STATE GUIDELINES, THE COURSE COULD BE MORE READILY GUIDED BY STUDENT INTEREST. ONE DAY, VERONICA AND TERI CAME IN SINGING TLC'S "WATERFALLS" AND I CHIMED IN...

YOU KNOW THAT SONG?

I DO HAVE A RADIO...

DID YOU KNOW THAT SONGS HAVE LICENSING FEES? LIKE IF YOU WANTED TO PUBLISH THOSE LYRICS IN A BOOK, YOU'D HAVE TO PAY A BUNCH OF MONEY.

FASCINATING!

WHAT DO YOU THINK THAT SONG'S ABOUT?

UH... WATERFALLS?

NOT QUITE. HOW ABOUT YOU EXAMINE THE LYRICS TONIGHT AND WE CAN DISCUSS THEIR MEANING IN CLASS?

THE NEXT DAY THE GIRLS CAME IN WITH THE MOST ENTHUSIASTIC RESPONSE I'D HAD TO AN ASSIGNMENT ALL SEMESTER.

AND IN THE 3RD VERSE...

MAYBE I SHOULD TRY THIS WITH THE OTHER KIDS...

I WORKED ON THE PROJECT THAT NIGHT.

YOU SHOULD EAT.

NOPE, IN THE ZONE.

THE IDEA WAS TO CHOOSE A MEANINGFUL SONG AND ANALYZE IT FOR THE CLASS.

ANY SONG?

ANY SONG, FRANKIE.

THE STUDENTS WERE EXPECTED TO BRING COPIES OF THEIR LYRICS IN FOR THE ENTIRE GROUP. THE NEXT DAY, I GOT A MESSAGE FROM PAM CRONIN, A TEACHER DOWN THE HALL.

YOU WANTED TO SEE ME?

FRANKIE ASKED ME TO PRINT COPIES OF THESE LYRICS FOR HIM...

I STARTED READING THEM AND I WAS JUST STUNNED. FRANKIE SAID YOU APPROVED IT, SO YOU CAN BE THE RESPONSIBLE FOR THE COPIES.

THE SONG WAS CALLED "BLOWJOB BETTY" AND IT ONLY GOT WORSE FROM THERE...

I LOOKED DUMB TWICE. FIRST TO PAM, THEN TO MY STUDENTS.

AS IT TURNS OUT, *ANY* SONG IS *NOT* OK...

THE ANALYSES THE KIDS DID VARIED WIDELY IN THEIR COMPLEXITY AND PRECEPTIVENESS.

WHEN HE SAYS HE'S "GOT 5 ON IT," HE MEANS 5 *DOLLARS*.

SOME STUDENTS REALLY SURPRISED ME.

WHAT COOLIO'S SAYING IS THAT A LOT OF TEACHERS CAN'T REALLY RELATE TO WHAT KIDS ARE GOING THROUGH 'CAUSE THEY COME FROM A DIFFERENT TYPE OF BACKGROUND.

SO HOW'S HE SUPPOSED TO GET HIS EDUCATION IF HIS TEACHERS DON'T EVEN UNDERSTAND HIM?

I SOMETIMES ENVY THOSE TEACHERS WHO ALWAYS SEEM SURE THEY'RE DOING THE RIGHT THING WITH THEIR STUDENTS...

BUT DESPITE LINGERING DOUBTS, I BELIEVE IN THE MEDIA STUDIES COURSE AND THE OPPORTUNITIES IT GIVES STUDENTS.

AND THAT'S WHY MEDIA STUDIES IS GREAT...

LEARNING TO VIEW TV AND OTHER MEDIA MORE CRITICALLY HELPS COMBAT FEELINGS OF POWERLESSNESS AND MARGINALIZATION.

I AM WORTH MY OPINION!

SOME TEACHERS MAY QUESTION WHETHER THE CLASS PROVIDES THE BASICS. SURE, THE KIDS ARE READING AND WRITING, BUT NOT MUCH.

WE'RE TAPING PROJECTS...

...DECONSTRUCTING CARTOONS...

...DISCUSSING HOMOPHOBIA.

I CAN'T SAY THAT EVERY STUDENT LEAVES WITH A BETTER UNDERSTANDING OF MASS COMMUNICATION AND ITS USES AND ABUSES. SOME DO, SOME DON'T.

I AM AWARE THAT, IF LATINO AND AFRICAN-AMERICAN CHILDREN ARE TO HAVE A CHANCE OF SUCCESS IN SOCIETY, THEY MUST BE TAUGHT SKILLS THAT SERVE THOSE ENDS.

BUT I CRINGE AT THE IDEA THAT MY STUDENTS NEED TO "GET BACK TO BASICS," AS IF THAT'S ALL THEY'RE CAPABLE OF.

NEW STUDIES SUGGEST NO!

I DON'T WANT TO ENDLESSLY DRILL THEM WITH BUSYWORK THAT LEAVES NO TIME FOR DOING OR MAKING THINGS, NO SPACE FOR REAL THOUGHT.

 STILL, I OFTEN WONDER IF WHAT I'M TEACHING MY KIDS IS MAKING ANY DIFFERENCE.

FINAL THOUGHT

 LATER THAT YEAR, A FEW STUDENTS ASKED ME TO ARRANGE A FIELD TRIP TO THE JERRY SPRINGER SHOW.

I THOUGHT IT COULD BE A GOOD WAY TO EXPOSE THE KIDS TO ITS EXCESSES. BUT I WORRIED IT MIGHT BACKFIRE.

 JERRY! JERRY! JERRY!

THE KIDS WOULDN'T LET THE IDEA DIE, THOUGH.

 PLEEEEEEASE...

COME ON, MR. MICHIE!

POST

PLEEEEEEASE!!!

FINALLY, I ORDERED TICKETS, SECRETLY HOPING FOR THE SLEAZIEST GABFEST EVER IN ORDER TO PROVE MY POINT.

JERRY'S GUESTS WERE TWO KIDS WITH HIV, AND THE ENTIRE SHOW WAS DEDICATED TO MAKING THEIR DREAMS COME TRUE.

 JERRY Springer

THE SHOW WAS STILL MANIPULATIVE, CALCULATED, AND SHALLOW, BUT MUCH OF THAT GOT BURIED BENEATH THE GLAMOROUS GUESTS, THE APPLAUSE, THE BRIGHT LIGHTS.

THE KIDS WITH HIV SEEMED HAPPY. JERRY LOOKED LIKE A HERO. WE ALL GOT CAUGHT UP IN THE CELEBRATORY ATMOSPHERE.

CHALK ONE UP FOR THE OPPOSITION.

FINAL THOUGHT

PALOMA

PALOMA, A 15-YEAR-OLD FRESHMAN, ATTENDS A HIGHLY REGARDED PUBLIC SCHOOL SEVERAL MILES SOUTH OF QUINCY. SHE HAS RECENTLY CELEBRATED HER QUINCEANERA––THE DAY, ACCORDING TO MEXICAN CATHOLIC TRADITION, WHEN A YOUNG WOMAN'S COMING OF AGE IS HONORED.

MY FATHER AND MOTHER ARE MY HEROES. MY FATHER HAD 14 BROTHERS AND SISTERS IN MEXICO, AND HIS MOTHER DIED WHEN HE WAS LITTLE.

HE DIDN'T HAVE MONEY FOR SCHOOL SO HE WORKED HARD AND GOT SCHOLARSHIPS, AND HE GRADUATED IN ENGINEERING.

NOW HE HAS HIS OWN CONSTRUCTION COMPANY.

MY MOTHER ONLY WENT TO SCHOOL TO 6TH GRADE. HER FAMILY HAD A FARM AND SHE WANTED TO HELP, SO SHE STOPPED GOING TO SCHOOL.

THEN SHE GOT MARRIED AND WANTED TO MAKE SURE SHE RAISED US WELL SO SHE DIDN'T GO BACK TO FINISH.

WHEN WE GOT OLDER WE FINALLY CONVINCED HER TO GO BACK TO SCHOOL, BECAUSE WE KNEW SHE WANTED TO.

WE WILL BE FINE.

SHE PASSED THE CONSTITUTION TEST, BECAME A CITIZEN, AND PASSED HER GED WITH A REALLY HIGH SCORE.

WE ARE PROUD OF YOU.

BECAUSE OF THE FAMILY I HAVE, I HAVE SUPPORT EVERYWHERE. THEY'VE NEVER LIMITED ME.

I DON'T THINK THE PROBLEMS OF MY GENERATION WERE CREATED BY US. THEY WERE BROUGHT ON BY PEOPLE WHO ARE OLDER.

YEAH, THERE'S A LOT OF KIDS OUT HERE DOING BAD THINGS. BUT REALLY, THERE ARE NO BAD KIDS.

PSA: DON'T BE A JERK! —Common sense

PEOPLE SAY IT'S A CHAIN. BECAUSE YOU GREW UP IN A CERTAIN NEIGHBORHOOD YOU'RE GONNA BE A CERTAIN WAY.

BUT I THINK IT DOESN'T HAVE TO BE THAT WAY. YOU DON'T HAVE TO BE JUST ANOTHER STATISTIC.

YOU CAN START YOUR OWN CHAIN--A GOOD ONE, YOU KNOW? BUT YOU CAN'T DO IT BY SITTING THERE DOING NOTHING. YOU HAVE TO CHANGE YOUR MENTALITY.

IT'S HARD WHEN THERE'S SO MANY NEGATIVE MESSAGES OUT THERE.

LIKE IF YOU SEE ON TV ALL THE TIME AFRICAN-AMERICAN OR LATINO KIDS IN GANGS, GETTING KILLED, GOING TO JAIL, AND YOU DON'T KNOW HOW TO BREAK IT DOWN, YOU'RE GONNA START THINKING THERE'S NO OTHER WAY.

LITTLE BY LITTLE IT GETS INTO YOUR HEAD UNLESS YOU ACTUALLY THINK ABOUT WHAT YOU'RE WATCHING.

WHEN I WATCH TV NOW, I LOOK FOR WHAT THEY'RE ACTUALLY TRYING TO SAY OR ASK MYSELF IF IT'S REALLY RELEVANT TO EVERYDAY LIFE.

THEY SAY THAT TV WASTES YOUR MIND, BUT YOU HAVE TO LOOK CLOSER AND WATCH IT MORE INTELLIGENTLY.

THE MOST IMPORTANT THING I LEARNED IN MEDIA STUDIES IS THAT I HAVE A VOICE IN SOCIETY.

CHILDREN ARE MINORITIES, TOO, NO MATTER WHAT RACE THEY ARE. SOME GROWN-UPS DON'T REALLY LISTEN TO KIDS.

PLEASE STOP AND LET'S REALLY TALK.

YOU DON'T HAVE TO BE RUDE, BUT EXPRESS YOUR FEELINGS, MAKE YOURSELF BE HEARD.

TRY TO REALLY LISTEN.

I'VE BEEN LUCKY. I'VE HAD TEACHERS WHO HAVE GIVEN ME INSPIRATION, WHO HAVE SHOWN ME I CAN BE SOMEBODY—NO MATTER MY COLOR, MY GENDER, MY RACE, AGE, WHATEVER.

LIKE MY HISTORY TEACHER—WHEN HE TEACHES, HE'S NOT WORRIED ABOUT GETTING THROUGH THE BOOK.

HE'S WORRIED ABOUT US UNDERSTANDING WHAT WE'RE READING. WHAT GOOD IS IT TO GET THROUGH THE WHOLE HISTORY BOOK WHEN THE KIDS DIDN'T LEARN ANYTHING?

IN ONE OF MY OTHER CLASSES, WE JUST COPY SECTIONS OF THE BOOK, WORD FOR WORD.

WE'RE JUST REWRITING THE BOOK. WHAT GOOD IS THAT?

I SAY ALL THE TIME I WANT TO MAKE A DIFFERENCE, BECAUSE I DO. MY APPROACH IS, I DO THINGS BEFORE SOMEBODY CAN STOP ME.

DON'T PUSH THE BUTTON!

SORRY, WHAT?

I JUST GO AHEAD AND DO IT. SOMEBODY MIGHT SAY

OH, YOU'RE A WOMAN. YOU CAN'T DO THIS.

BUT I'LL BE LIKE, "SORRY, I ALREADY DID IT."

SEE IF I CARE

ILLUSTRATED BY DALIN DOHRN

THAT NIGHT I GRADED PAPERS WHILE FEELING LIKE AN IDIOT ABOUT MY OUTBURST.

I REALIZED MY REACTION WAS AS MUCH ABOUT MY OWN EXHAUSTION AS IT WAS ABOUT MY STUDENTS' APPARENT INDIFFERENCE.

IT WASN'T THAT THEY DIDN'T CARE. MAYBE THEY THOUGHT THEIR CARING WOULDN'T MAKE A DIFFERENCE.

MY THOUGHTS TURNED TO 12-YEAR-OLD SAMUEL DE LA CRUZ, ONE OF MY STUDENTS WHO NEVER SEEMED TO GIVE A DAMN.

PBBT

WHEN HIS HOMEROOM TEACHER, MS. REILLY, ANNOUNCED TO THE CLASS THAT SHE WAS PLANNING TO QUIT DUE TO THEIR BEHAVIOR, I COULDN'T IMAGINE SAMUEL GIVING IT A SECOND THOUGHT.

BUT AFTER I READ THE WORDS HE PENNED IN MY WRITING CLASS, I NEVER LOOKED AT HIM THE SAME WAY.

Dear miss Reilly,
I want to tell you that your a Great teacher, but i know that i dont Pay attenchen. Sorry that i get in troble. But you know what, I could Help you. Its like God send me. Im going to give you some Pointers. Let the children Play and Learn. Like with the flash cards. I am doing this four you and the students not just four me. just give it a try for us Dont quit on us, Please miss Reilly we Really care about you. You Dont have to waste Your Anergy and you will be happy. by the way we care about you.
      X SAMUEL DELA CRUZ

RUBY ANAYA DIDN'T CARE MUCH, EITHER.

AT LEAST THAT'S WHAT HER SCIENCE TEACHER, MR. SHEPHERD, THOUGHT.

WHAT'S HE EVEN TALKING ABOUT?

LIFE HAS RULES, PLAY FAIR.

TODAYS HW: P.293

$12V$ $\Omega: ?$ $I=?$

I'VE HAD ABOUT ENOUGH OF YOUR MOUTH! I'VE BEEN TEACHING LONGER THAN YOU'VE BEEN ALIVE, YOUNG LADY!

THAT DON'T MAKE NO SENSE.

OUT! GO SEE MS. HOSKINS!

MS. HOSKINS WAS A DISCIPLINARIAN WITH A NOVEL APPROACH: SHE LISTENED TO KIDS.

WHAT HAPPENED, HONEY?

HE DON'T LISTEN TO ME.

IT SOUNDS LIKE BOTH PARTIES COULD DO SOME IMPROVING. WHAT DO YOU THINK?

YEAH...

WHY DON'T YOU TRY WRITING ABOUT HOW EACH OF YOU CAN IMPROVE? BRING IT IN AND WE'LL DISCUSS IT.

OK.

MAYBE MR. SHEPHERD WOULD BE INTERESTED IN READING IT, TOO.

YEAH, RIGHT...

How we could Improve
By Ruby Anaya
If we want to improve ourselves, we must understand each other. I think teachers should try to make school fun. the kids should pay more attention and not act dum. and not get in alot of trouble. I think if we want to improve we need to get our minds together. some teachers need to stop having a high temper and stop blaming the kids. I would like to improve myself, but there is some people that make me mad and makes me think that maybe it is not worth it. I think we could improve but we must have a little-help. All parents, teachers, and especially us children must put forth some effort.

UNFORTUNATELY, NEITHER RUBY'S NOR SAMUEL'S LETTERS MADE MUCH OF AN IMPACT.

ALTHOUGH SHE DIDN'T GO THROUGH WITH HER PREMATURE RETIREMENT PLAN, MS. REILLY LAUGHED OFF SAMUEL'S PROPOSAL.

CUTE.

MS. REILLY

AS FAR AS I KNOW, MR. SHEPHERD NEVER EVEN READ WHAT RUBY WROTE.

YEARS EARLIER, HE'D BEEN A BELOVED 3RD GRADE TEACHER.

IMAGINE!

WE LOVE MR. SHEPH

3R

WHAT HAD CHANGED? WAS IT MR. SHEPHERD? THE STUDENTS? THE WORLD?

A FEW WEEKS LATER...

SO...

HOW DO YOU GUYS FEEL ABOUT THE METAL DETECTORS?

IT'S LIKE WE'RE CRIMINALS! LIKE WE'RE ON LOCKDOWN!

I GOT PATTED DOWN!

I MEAN, IF IT MAKES THE SCHOOL SAFER...

THEY THINK EVERY KID IN THIS NEIGHBORHOOD'S A GANGBANGER!

THE DISCUSSION WAS LIVELY AND ANIMATED. STUDENTS VOICED THEIR OPINIONS.

...AT LEAST, MOST OF THEM...

BRINNNNNG

MAYRA, CAN I TALK WITH YOU AFTER SCHOOL?

MAYRA HAD ALWAYS BEEN AN EXCELLENT STUDENT. SHE DIDN'T QUITE FIT IN WITH THE OTHER KIDS, BUT SHE WAS BRIGHT AND INSIGHTFUL.

THOUGH HER CONTRIBUTIONS TO CLASS WERE INFREQUENT, HER OBSERVATIONS WERE KEEN.

IN THE LAST MONTH, SHE'D BEEN COMING TO CLASS LESS, AND WHEN SHE WAS THERE, HER MIND WAS OBVIOUSLY ELSEWHERE.

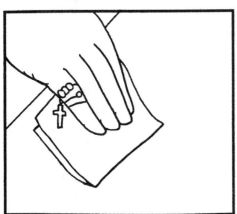

days and nights seem to pass by slowly and I still can't get myself together so many times I tell myself that it's going to get better and its all in the past but everything is one dark cloud of mist, and I'm in the middle trying to find my way out. once there was a helping hand that was guiding me out of the mist but the hand let go, and I was taken back into the middle, lost in the depths of mist once again

SHE DON'T LISTEN TO ME.

WHO DOESN'T LISTEN?

MY MA.

SHE IGNORES ME. SHE DON'T EVEN UNDERSTAND WHAT IT'S LIKE TO BE A KID 'CAUSE SHE GOT MARRIED WHEN SHE WAS 14.

SHE THINKS EVERYTHING'S MY FAULT.

LIKE WHAT?

EVERYTHING.

WELL, WHAT'S EVERYTHING?

SOMETHING'S GOING ON, MAYRA. I CAN TELL. YOU'VE BEEN LIKE A DIFFERENT PERSON THESE PAST FEW WEEKS.

...IT'S MY DAD.

I SAW HIM LIKE A MONTH AGO.

I HID FROM HIM. I DIDN'T WANT HIM TO SEE ME.

BUT THEN THAT NIGHT, ALL THESE MEMORIES CAME FLOODING BACK.

GRADUALLY, MAYRA BEGAN TO TELL ME A PART OF HER STORY THAT I'D NEVER HEARD BEFORE.

MY FATHER AND MOTHER WORKED IN THE SAME TAMALE FACTORY.

HE WORKED 1ST SHIFT, SHE WORKED 3RD.

SOME NIGHTS, HE'D COME INTO OUR ROOM.

DO NOT TELL YOUR MOTHER.

AFTER YEARS OF THIS, MY AUNT FIGURED OUT WHAT WAS HAPPENING. SHE TREATENED TO CALL THE POLICE.

MY MOM DEFENDED HIM. SHE BLAMED US WHEN HE LEFT.

SLAM

WE NEVER TALKED ABOUT IT. I TRIED TO FORGET. THEN, WHEN I SAW HIM...

WHAT SHOULD I STAY IN SCHOOL FOR? THEY DON'T CARE IF I FINISH. THEY DON'T CARE ABOUT ME.

RUBY ⭐

RUBY HAD HER 1ST CHILD AT 15. NOW 17, SHE LIVES WITH HER BOYFRIEND AND 2 CHILDREN JUST A STONE'S THROW FROM QUINCY.

THAT STUFF ABOUT CUTTING WELFARE PISSES ME OFF. I THINK EVERY KID SHOULD HAVE A MEDICAL CARD TO HELP WITH THE HOSPITAL BILLS AND STUFF.

IT'S GONNA AFFECT WOMEN THE MOST, BECAUSE A MAN CAN HAVE AS MANY KIDS AS HE WANTS, BUT HE CAN JUST LEAVE.

FOR ME, THE HARDEST PART OF BEING A MOTHER IS TAKING MY KIDS TO THE DOCTOR. I DON'T LIKE TO SEE THEM CRY WHEN THEY GET THEIR SHOTS OR KNOW THAT THEY'RE GOING TO BE HURTING.

IT'S HARD TO BE PATIENT SOMETIMES, TOO. SOMETIMES I FEEL LIKE THEY BOTHER ME, LIKE THEY'RE IN MY WAY. I'VE EVEN SAID THAT TO THEM.

BUT WHEN I DO, I SAY, "I'M SORRY, I DIDN'T MEAN THAT," AND THEY UNDER-STAND. LITTLE KIDS ARE A LOT SMARTER THAN PEOPLE THINK THEY ARE.

I REMEMBER BEING TOLD I WASN'T A GOOD DAUGHTER, THAT I WASN'T GOOD ENOUGH TO BE IN THE FAMILY. I HEARD IT FROM MY MOTHER'S MOUTH, AND IT STILL HURTS.

I'M TRYING TO RAISE MY KIDS THE WAY I WOULD'VE WANTED TO BE RAISED. IF YOU HAD A SAD CHILDHOOD, YOU'RE GOING TO TRY TO MAKE YOUR KIDS' DIFFERENT.

I STILL THINK THE WAY I DID IN 8TH GRADE. WOMEN SHOULD HAVE EQUAL OPPORTUNITIES IN EVERYTHING, IN EVERY WAY.

MY STANDARD IS STILL THE SAME. BUT ONCE A BABY IS BORN, THE FEELINGS OF A WOMAN CHANGE.

I HAVE DECIDED TO STAY HOME, BECAUSE IT'S HARD FOR ME TO WORK. I HAVE NO BABYSITTER.

BUT IF A WOMAN WANTS TO WORK, IT SHOULD BE HER DECISION, TOO. THE HUSBAND SHOULDN'T TELL HER SHE CAN'T.

A LOT OF MEXICAN MEN THINK THE WOMAN SHOULD JUST STAY IN THE HOUSE ALL DAY. BUT THOSE MEN SHOULD GET A MAID, BECAUSE A WOMAN IS NOT A SLAVE.

SOME TEACHERS WOULD TELL US

HEY, YOU CAN DO SOME-THING WITH YOUR LIFE.

ⓐ their
ⓑ there
ⓒ they're

BUT I'M PRETTY SURE THAT WHEN THEY WOULD COME OUT OF SCHOOL, THEY WOULD THINK

SHE'S A SLOW STUDENT. SHE'S NEVER GONNA DO ANYTHING.

ROOM 205

YOU COULD FEEL THAT THEY WERE LYING TO YOU, YOU KNOW?

ONE OF MY TEACHERS EVEN COMPARED US TO HIS DOGS. HE WOULD TELL US HIS DOGS COULD DO SOMETHING THAT WE COULDN'T DO.

BE A WINNER NOT A WHINER

$$\left(\frac{a}{b}\right)^m = \frac{a^m}{b^m}$$
$$b \neq 0$$

BUT THERE WERE SOME TEACHERS WHO WERE DIFFERENT, LIKE MR. Z.

HE WOULD LOOK INTO YOUR EYES AND REALLY TALK TO YOU. HE DIDN'T TEACH THE HIGH GROUPS ANY DIFFERENT FROM THE LOW GROUPS.

I THINK MR. Z WOULD TEACH SCHOOL EVEN IF HE DIDN'T GET PAID.

I THINK KIDS REALLY DO CARE. IN THE BOTTOM OF THEIR HEARTS, THEY DO.

BUT IT DEPENDS ON BOTH SIDES. THE KID HAS TO LISTEN TO THE TEACHER, BUT THE TEACHER HAS TO LISTEN TO THE KID, TOO.

IN A WAY, THE STUDENT SHOULD BE A STUDENT-TEACHER AND THE TEACHER SHOULD BE A TEACHER-STUDENT.

YOU GOTTA BE HARD

THE ANNUAL BACK OF THE YARDS INDEPENDENCIA DE MEXICO PARADE IS AN OPPORTUNITY FOR THE NEIGHBORHOOD'S RESIDENTS TO COME TOGETHER.

FAMILIES COME OUT TO SHOW THEIR PRIDE.

¡VIVA MEXICO!

¡VIIIIIII-VAAA!

COMMUNITY LEADERS, SUCH AS FATHER BRUCE WELLEMS, JOIN THE FESTIVITIES.

I STOOD BESIDE AHMED, A STUDENT WHOSE PALESTINIAN HERITAGE MADE HIM ONE OF QUINCY'S FEW NON-MEXICAN STUDENTS.

I DON'T GET IT...

IT WASN'T THE DISPLAY OF CULTURAL PRIDE THAT AHMED DIDN'T GET. IT WAS THE CEREMONIAL SHOW OF FORCE DISPLAYED BY 2 RIVAL GANGS HAPPENING ON THE SIDE-LINES.

JESTER LOVE, MUTHAFUCKA!

THAT'S NOT GONNA HAPPEN TO ME. AIN'T NO WAY. THIS KID'S NOT GOING THAT ROUTE.

ILLUSTRATED BY CITLALI PEREZ

I'D HEARD A SIMILAR PRONOUNCEMENT FROM LUIS BRAVO 3 YEARS EARLIER.

HIS EASY CHARM MADE HIM A SHOO-IN FOR PRESIDENT OF THE STUDENT COUNCIL AND CAPTAIN OF QUINCY'S BASKETBALL TEAM.

HIS OLDER BROTHER WAS A MEMBER OF THE JESTERS, AND LUIS WAS FEELING THE PRESSURE TO FOLLOW SUIT.

IN JANUARY, HE SHAVED HIS HEAD, A SIGNAL HE MIGHT "TURN."

IN MARCH, AFTER TAGGING ON A SCHOOL BUS, HE WAS KICKED OFF THE BASKETBALL TEAM AND STUDENT COUNCIL.

IN FEBRUARY, HE WAS SUSPENDED FOR FIGHTING.

HE DROPPED OUT OF SCHOOL EARLY THE NEXT YEAR, WAS ARRESTED SOON AFTER, AND ENDED UP FLEEING TO MEXICO, ALLEGEDLY DUE TO A MURDER CHARGE.

AHMED KNEW LUIS' STORY. HE KNEW HOW HARD IT WAS TO AVOID THE TRAGIC UNDERTOW OF GANG INVOLVEMENT. EVEN I KNEW THAT.

WHEN I STARTED TEACHING, I FELT I WAS IN DIRECT COMPETITION WITH STREET GANGS FOR THE HEARTS AND MINDS OF MY STUDENTS. ME AGAINST THEM.

I REALIZED THAT MY OUTLOOK WAS SHAPED BY A STEADY DIET OF GANG-RELATED HORROR STORIES FROM THE CHICAGO MEDIA.

Chicago

BUT THAT REALIZATION DIDN'T MAKE THE REPORTS OF VIOLENCE ANY LESS FRIGHTENING, OR THE ISSUE OF GANGS ANY EASIER TO FIGURE OUT.

A MONTH OR SO AFTER I MADE MARVELOUS SCRUB THAT DESK, I NOTICED HIM TAUNTING ANOTHER STUDENT IN THE HALLWAY DURING A PASSING PERIOD.

HE AND HIS EVER-PRESENT SHADOW, KHAN, APPROACHED A KID NAMED WILLIAM AS A CROWD GATHERED...

P LOVE!

WHAT UP?

SUDDENLY MOSES GREEN, AN 8TH GRADE MATH TEACHER WHOM THE KIDS CALLED PREACHER, APPEARED.

MARVELOUS JENKINS AND KHANTRELL DAVIS, YOU BETTER GET UP OFFA THAT BOY!

I DONE TOLD YOU FELLAS ABOUT REPRESENTIN' IN THIS SCHOOL.

IN THE AFTERMATH OF THE FIGHT, THE REST OF THE DAY WAS UNPRODUCTIVE. HEADING HOME AFTER CLASS, I PASSED MR. GREEN'S ROOM.

ALTHOUGH HE WAS ADAMANTLY OPPOSED TO GANG CULTURE, HE WAS ABLE TO EMOTIONALLY AND INTELLECTUALLY SEPARATE THE INSTITUTION FROM THE INDIVIDUALS.

HE LISTENED TO THEM. HE RELATED TO THEM AS PEOPLE. AS HE WORKED WITH THEM TO RESOLVE THEIR DIFFERENCES, HE DIDN'T SEE 3 GANGBANGERS. HE SAW WILLIAM, MARVELOUS, AND KHAN.

GRADUALLY, I BEGAN TO SEE THEM, TOO.

I MADE A CONSCIOUS EFFORT TO GET TO KNOW MARVELOUS AND KHAN BETTER.

I LOVE THIS DRAWING! YOU SHOULD SUBMIT IT TO THE SCHOOL NEWSPAPER.

YEAH?

AS WE BECAME COMFORTABLE WITH EACH OTHER, THEY GAVE ME INFORMAL LESSONS.

THE MAD DISCIPLES AINT A GANG, IT'S AN ORGANIZATION.

THE MD STANDS FOR MATURITY AND DEVELOPMENT.

WILLIAM, ON THE OTHER HAND, NEVER REALLY OPENED UP TO ME ON A PERSONAL LEVEL.

ON THE DAYS HE CAME TO CLASS, HE WAS ALOOF, CAREFULLY MAINTAINING HIS "HARD" EXTERIOR.

Y'ALL SOME IGN'ANT MU'FUCKAS.

STILL, HE RARELY FAILED TO TURN IN A COMPOSITION ASSIGNMENT, AND HIS WRITING UNVEILED A SENSITIVITY AND COMPASSION THAT BETRAYED HIS GANGSTER POSES.

I JUST GET THESE VISIONS AND I WRITE 'EM DOWN, THAT'S ALL.

WELL, YOU'RE PRETTY GOOD AT IT.

...THANKS.

AT QUINCY, THE NEIGHBORHOOD GANG WAS THE LATIN JESTERS.

FEW KIDS WERE MEMBERS, BUT MANY FELT THE HEAT OF INTIMIDATION.

IF I GO TO THE PARK, THEY'RE ALWAYS THERE TELLIN' ME, "YOU'RE A PUNK. WHY DON'T YOU TURN?"

INITIALLY I AVOIDED THE TOPIC IN CLASS BECAUSE I FELT I'D BE GIVING THE GANG ADDITIONAL EXPOSURE.

HOWEVER, THE MORE TIME I SPENT IN THE COMMUNITY, THE MORE I REALIZED THE JESTER'S PRESENCE WAS INESCAPABLE.

SO, I BEGAN TRYING TO CREATE OPPORTUNITIES FOR STUDENTS TO EXPRESS THEIR FEELINGS ABOUT GROWING UP AROUND--OR WITHIN--GANG CULTURE.

I WANT EACH OF YOU TO WRITE ONE PARAGRAPH ABOUT SOMETHING POSITIVE YOU SEE IN YOUR NEIGHBORHOOD, AND ONE ABOUT SOMETHING NEGATIVE.

I LIKE THE PUBLIC LIBRARY BECAUSE IT'S CALM AND PEACEFUL.

MY FAVORITE THING ABOUT THE NEIGHBORHOOD IS THE CHURCH BECAUSE IT IS NICE AND BIG. IT BRINGS BACK A LOT OF MEMORIES.

THE MOST UNIQUE OFFERING CAME FROM 12-YEAR-OLD LUIS BRAVO.

ONE POSITIVE THING IS AT THE PARK, THERE ARE WOOD CHIPS ALL AROUND THE SWINGS, SO WHEN KIDS SLIP AND FALL, THEY DON'T GET HURT.

THE KIDS SPOKE ALMOST IN UNISON WHEN IT CAME TO CITING A NEGATIVE ELEMENT.

I DON'T LIKE THE PARK BECAUSE THERE ARE A LOT OF GANGS THERE.

THE GRAFFITTI IS UGLY. IF PEOPLE KEEP REMOVING IT, MAYBE GANGSTERS WOULD GET TIRED OF WRITING IT.

A LOT OF ACCIDENTS HAPPEN BECAUSE OF GANGSTERS FIGHTING.

THAT FRIDAY WE WENT OUTSIDE TO VIDEOTAPE FOOTAGE TO ACCOMPANY THEIR WRITTEN NARRATIVES.

°REC

THAT WAS COOL, MR. MICHIE.

WE SHOULD COME OUTSIDE EVERY DAY.

GOING OUTSIDE EVERYDAY WAS IMPRACTICAL, BUT I TRIED TO BRING WHAT WAS GOING ON OUTSIDE INTO CLASS.

DO YOU THINK THE POLICE ARE DEALING WITH THE GANG'S ACTIVITIES?

NO!

WELL, SOME ARE AND SOME AREN'T.

THE COPS ARE NEVER AROUND WHEN YOU NEED 'EM. ONLY WHEN YOU DON'T.

YEAH, RIGHT HERE THE POLICE JUST PASS BY. THEY DON'T DO ANYTHING!

WHAT DO YOU WANT THEM TO DO?

I DON'T KNOW...

THAT SPRING, I ASSIGNED MY MEDIA STUDIES CLASS THE TASK OF WRITING TO MAYOR RICHARD M. DALEY.

YOU REALLY THINK HE'S GONNA READ 'EM?

I DON'T KNOW. BUT THE IMPORTANT THING IS THAT YOU SPEAK UP.

HE'S PROBABLY BUSY.

HE MAY HAVE SOMEONE READ THEM FOR HIM.

WELL, THEY *BETTER* READ MINE.

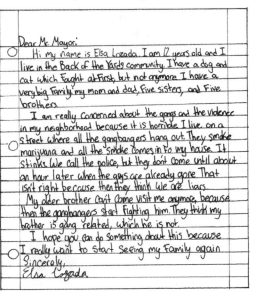

Dear Mr. Mayor:
   Hi my name is Elsa Lozada. I am 12 years old and I live in the Back of the Yards community. I have a dog and cat which Fought at First, but not anymore. I have a very big Family; my mom and dad, Five sisters, and Five brothers.
   I am really concerned about the gangs and the violence in my neighborhood because it is horrible. I live on a street where all the gangbangers hang out. They smoke marijuana and all the smoke comes in to my house. It stinks. We call the police, but they don't come until about an hour later when the guys are already gone. That isn't right because then they think we are liars.
   My older brother can't come visit me anymore, because then the gangbangers start fighting him. They think my brother is gang related, which he is not.
   I hope you can do something about this because I really want to start seeing my Family again.
Sincerely,
Elsa Lozada

I WAS SURPRISED TO RECEIVE A REPLY WEEKS LATER THAT WAS SPECIFICALLY TAILORED TO THE KIDS' CONCERNS. I HUNG IT ON THE BULLETIN BOARD BUT THE KIDS WERE UNIMPRESSED. THE BIGGEST REACTION WAS TO THE MAYOR'S SIGNATURE.

DAMN, HE WRITES NASTY.

AND HE'S THE *MAYOR?*

PERHAPS THE MOST POWERFUL STATEMENTS MY STUDENTS MADE ON GANGS CAME IN THE FORM OF DRAMATIC VIDEO PRODUCTIONS.

VIDEOTAPED "DIALOGUE POEMS" ARE DESIGNED TO PRESENT DIFFERENT PERSPECTIVES ON AN ISSUE, SUCH AS THE COMMUNICATION BREAKDOWN BETWEEN A MOTHER AND SON IN, "I HAVE A FEELING."

PEPE IS MY ONLY CHILD.

I AM THE ONLY ONE.

I LOVE MY KID.

MY MA DOESN'T LOVE ME.

BUT MY CHILD HAS CHANGED.

I'M A GANG MEMBER.

HE HAS PROBLEMS.

I SELL DRUGS.

I WANT TO TALK TO HIM.

I DON'T WANT TO LISTEN.

HE STAYS OUT LATE EVERY NIGHT.

I DON'T WANNA GO HOME.

HE'S HAVING PROBLEMS.

WHAT IS HAPPENING TO ME?

I HAVE A FEELING...

...SOMETHING BAD IS GOING TO HAPPEN.

KIDS PRODUCED A LOT OF INSIGHTFUL WORK. STILL, AS ONE OF MY STUDENTS USED TO ALWAYS ASK:

WHAT'S THE POINT?

THE VIDEOS, THE LETTERS, THE POEMS... HAVE THEY RAISED AWARENESS? MADE A DIFFERENCE? OR HAVE THEY JUST BEEN SCHOOL ASSIGNMENTS?

THE TRUTH IS, IT'S HARD TO TELL. THE SAME KIDS PORTRAYING GANGBANGERS IN OUR VIDEOS ARE SOMETIMES PLAYING THE ROLES FOR REAL A SHORT TIME LATER.

AS THEY GROW INTO THEIR TEENS, MANY COME TO REALIZE THE AMERICAN DREAM IS A TEXTBOOK FABLE. AS THEY COME TO FEEL THEIR OPTIONS NARROWING, THE GANG CULTURE AROUND THEM LOOMS LARGER AND LARGER.

WHEN THEY FINALLY JOIN, IT'S NOT SO MUCH A CHOICE AS A SURRENDER. AN ACKNOWLEDGEMENT THAT, IN THEIR EYES, THERE ARE NO OTHER CHOICES LEFT.

YET THE MAJORITY OF KIDS IN BACK OF THE YARDS RESIST THE TEMPTATION. BUT IT ISN'T EASY.

IT'S MESSED UP OUT THERE. IF THEY THINK YOU'RE SOFT, THEY'LL TRY TO MESS WITH YOU. YOU GOTTA BE HARD.

CONNECTING WITH KIDS WHO TURN TO GANGS AND CREATING OPPORTUNITIES FOR THEM CAN HELP THEM MAKE BETTER CHOICES. JUST ASK FATHER BRUCE, WHO HAS WORKED EXTENSIVELY WITH GANG-INVOLVED YOUTH IN BACK OF THE YARDS.

EVERYBODY WANTS A RULEBOOK ON HOW TO RELATE TO GANGBANGERS, BUT NOBODY WANTS TO RELATE TO THEM.

WE HAVE TO TRY TO EDUCATE THEM SO THEY BECOME MORE CONSCIOUS OF THEIR CHOICES. WE HAVE TO UNDERSTAND THESE KIDS AS PEOPLE WITH BASIC NEEDS THAT AREN'T BEING ANSWERED.

THE TEMPTATION IS TO LOOK AT THESE GUYS AND PUT EVERYTHING IN BLACK AND WHITE. BUT WHEN IS ANYTHING BLACK AND WHITE? IT JUST ISN'T.

JUAN, 17, DREAMS OF BEING A FILM DIRECTOR. BUT HE HAS GROWN DISENCHANTED WITH SCHOOL AND FALLEN BEHIND ON HIS CREDITS. IT'S BEGINNING TO LOOK DOUBTFUL THAT HE'LL GRADUATE ON TIME, IF AT ALL.

I GUESS YOU COULD SAY I WAS ONE OF THE LUCKY ONES. GANGBANGING NEVER REALLY CAUGHT MY ATTENTION.

WHEN I WAS YOUNGER, I WAS AFRAID THAT IF I JOINED A GANG, MY DAD WAS GONNA KILL ME.

THEN, AT QUINCY, I WAS IN THE VIDEO PROGRAM SO I HAD SOMETHING TO DO AFTER SCHOOL. AND THE DAY I GRADUATED FROM 8TH GRADE MY MOM TOOK ME TO GET A JOB. SO THOSE WERE MY PRIORITIES--WORKING AND GOING TO SCHOOL.

I THINK WHAT WORRIES ME MOST IN MY LIFE IS THE ECONOMY.

I'M BROKE AS A JOKE. I MEAN, IT'S LIKE, WHEN YOU GOT MONEY, IT'S NOT EVEN THERE.

DAMN, I WISH I HAD 5 BUCKS.

BUT THEN WHEN YOU HAVE THE $5, IT'S NOT ENOUGH. YOU WANT MORE.

I MAKE $60 A WEEK CLEANING THE WINDOWS AT THE LAUNDROMAT...

15 GOES TO BUS TOKENS, 15 I GIVE TO MY GRAND-MOTHER, AND 15 I GIVE TO MY MA.

SO THAT LEAVES ME $15 FOR 2 WEEKS. THAT'S A DOLLAR A DAY. THAT SUCKS.

SOME PEOPLE SAY WE GOT EQUAL OPPORTUNITIES IN THIS COUNTRY...

BUT I THINK IT DEPENDS ON WHAT IT IS YOU'RE TRYING TO DO. AND WHO'S IN CHARGE. IS IT A WHITE GUY IN CHARGE?

I THINK I GET DISCRIMINATED BECAUSE OF THE COLOR OF MY SKIN. I THINK BLACK PEOPLE HAVE IT THE WORST. AND WOMEN HAVE IT BAD, TOO.

I REMEMBER ONE TIME IN 3RD GRADE, I WAS SITTING IN CLASS WONDERING WHO IT WAS THAT INVENTED SCHOOL.

IT MUST HAVE BEEN SOMEBODY WHO HATED KIDS...

THE WAY I LOOK AT IT, TEACHERS ARE STRICT 'CAUSE THEY'RE AFRAID OF THEIR STUDENTS.

FOR EXAMPLE, MY ENGLISH TEACHER. I KNOW SHE KNOWS WHAT SHE'S DOING, BUT IT'S THE WAY SHE APPROACHES IT THAT KILLS THE CLASS.

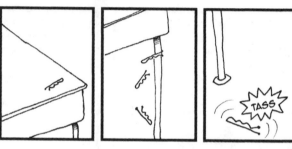

TASS

IT'S SO QUIET IN THERE 'CAUSE EVERY-BODY'S AFRAID OF HER.

GASP

I WANT TO BE A RESPECTED MAN. A MAN OF INTEGRITY.

IN A WAY I FEEL SCARED BECAUSE IF I DON'T MAKE IT IN BECOMING A DIRECTOR, THE ONLY THING LEFT FOR ME IS DOING WHAT MY DAD DOES-- ROOFING. AND THAT'S KIND OF MESSED UP.

IT'S LIKE MY DREAM COULD COME CRASHING DOWN, YOU KNOW? EVERYTHING.

And Justice For Some

AS SOON AS I ROUNDED THE CORNER, I KNEW SOMETHING WAS WRONG.

WHAT'S THE MATTER? AREN'T YOU GUYS EXCITED FOR THE GAME?

JOANNE MACIAS, A TEACHER'S AIDE AT QUINCY, WAS THE FIRST TO REPLY.

IT'S REGGIE...

HE JUST GOT ATTACKED BY A COP.

THE FIRST TIME I MET REGGIE WILSON WAS 2 YEARS EARLIER, WHEN HE WAS IN 6TH GRADE.

ILLUSTRATED BY AUGUST ABITANG AND TATUM HOWLETT

OH, SORRY, I'LL COME BACK LATER...

THAT'S OK, WE WERE JUST FINISHING UP.

REGGIE, HAVE YOU MET MR. MICHIE?

HI.

WE'LL TALK ABOUT THIS SOME MORE TOMORROW, REGGIE. JUST TRY NOT TO LET WHAT THEY SAY GET TO YOU, OK?

OK.

THANK YOU, MS. HOSKINS.

WHAT'S HAPPENING WITH HIM?

I DON'T KNOW EXACTLY. HE'S BEEN ACTING OUT IN CLASS LATELY. NOTHING MAJOR, BUT IT KEEPS HAPPENING.

I THINK HE'S DOING IT TO GET ACCEPTANCE FROM THE OTHER BOYS. SOME OF THEM HAVE BEEN GIVING HIM A HARD TIME. NAME-CALLING...

RACIAL?

OUT OF THE 900 KIDS AT QUINCY, 3 WERE AFRICAN-AMERICAN. REGGIE WAS THE ONLY BLACK STUDENT IN THE UPPER GRADES.

SOME OF IT. BUT SOME OF IT IS JUST THE BULLY THING.

THEY SEE HE DOESN'T FIGHT BACK SO THEY PICK ON HIM. REGGIE HAS VERY LOW SELF-ESTEEM.

HE'S VERY QUIET. NOT ASSERTIVE AT ALL. THAT'S PROBABLY ONE OF THE REASONS THEY'RE DOING HIM LIKE THEY ARE.

REGGIE'S TOO NICE FOR HIS OWN GOOD. HE'S AN EASY TARGET.

REGGIE, ARE YOU ALL RIGHT?

YEAH...

HI, MR. MICHIE.

DO YOU WANT ME TO TAKE YOU HOME?

I STILL WANT TO GO TO THE GAME.

IT'S THE CHAMPIONSHIP. I WANT TO BE THERE WITH THE OTHER GUYS.

WHAT HAPPENED?

WE WERE STANDING THERE ON THE CORNER, WAITING FOR THE BUS...

DAVE CORONADO, QUINCY'S BASKETBALL COACH, ARRIVED A FEW MINUTES LATER. WE AGREED TO REPORT WHAT HAD TAKEN PLACE.

I CALLED THE POLICE DEPARTMENT AND WAS ASSURED THAT MY SECONDHAND ACCOUNT OF THE OFFICER'S BRUTALITY HAD BEEN FILED.

DAVE, WHO HAD SPENT HIS ENTIRE LIFE ON THE SOUTH SIDE, WAS SKEPTICAL.

AFTER THE GAME, HE TOOK REGGIE, REGGIE'S MOTHER, MS. MACIAS, AND 2 STUDENT WITNESSES DOWN TO THE PRECINCT TO FILE A REPORT IN PERSON.

JUST TO BE SURE.

HEY, THIS IS CHICAGO.

BETWEEN THE TIME I MET HIM AND THE INCIDENT, I'D GOTTEN TO KNOW REGGIE PRETTY WELL.

IT WASN'T JUST HIS SKIN COLOR THAT SET REGGIE APART AT QUINCY. HE SEEMED TO MOVE IN AN ORBIT ALL HIS OWN.

HE WAS AN UNUSUALLY POLITE KID. HIS UNASSUMING NATURE TENDED TO MASK HIS EMOTIONS. HIS LAUGHTER, LIKE HIS ANGER, WAS SUBDUED.

HE WAS A '90'S KID WITH '60'S SENSIBILITIES, PREFERRING "OLD SCHOOL," RHYTHM AND BLUES: STEVIE WONDER, AL GREEN, MARVIN GAYE...

MUSIC PROVIDED OUR FIRST REAL CONNECTION. WHEN I LEARNED FROM ONE OF HIS ESSAYS THAT HIS FAVORITE BAND WAS EARTH, WIND & FIRE, I MENTIONED HAVING ALL OF THEIR ALBUMS AT HOME.

REGGIE SEEMED AMAZED THAT WE SHARED AN INTEREST. BEFORE LONG, I WAS MAKING HIM TAPES OF OLD ALBUMS, AND WE WERE COMPARING NOTES ON FAVORITE TUNES.

ONE DAY, WHEN I WAS LEAVING SCHOOL...

HEY MR. MICHIE! I'VE BEEN PRACTICING. I THINK I'VE GOT IT DOWN.

PRACTICING WHAT?

"FANTASY." WANNA HEAR IT?

"FANTASY" WAS REGGIE'S FAVORITE EARTH, WIND & FIRE SONG.

SURE. YOU WANNA SING IT RIGHT HERE?

I WAS ASTONISHED. A YEAR EARLIER, THIS KID COULD BARELY LOOK ME IN THE EYE.

A COUPLE WEEKS AFTER WE REPORTED THE OFFICER, REGGIE'S MOTHER GOT A LETTER STATING THAT THE POLICE DEPARTMENT WOULD CONDUCT AN 'IMMEDIATE AND THOROUGH' INVESTIGATION.

THEY TOLD ME THE PROCESS WOULD TAKE SEVERAL MONTHS.

SOMETIMES THESE INVESTIGATIONS GET DRAWN OUT SO LONG, THE VICTIMS JUST MOVE ON WITH THEIR LIVES.

THE STAFF AT QUINCY WAS EAGER TO GET INVOLVED. BUT HOW? WHAT COULD WE DO? I CALLED *THE CHICAGO DEFENDER*, AN HISTORICALLY BLACK NEWSPAPER WITH A HISTORY OF SPEAKING OUT AGAINST RACIAL INJUSTICE.

THEY SENT A REPORTER TO THE SCHOOL TO INTERVIEW REGGIE AND THE WITNESSES.

AN ARTICLE HEADLINED "STUDENT SHOCKED BY BEATING: POLICE OFFICER ALLEGEDLY BRUTALIZES TEEN" RAN ON PAGE 3 THE NEXT DAY.

THAT SAME WEEK, I HAPPENED TO BE AT THE STUDIOS OF WMAQ-TV, CHAPERONING A STUDENT VIDEO CREW.

WHILE WE WERE THERE, I TOLD A REPORTER ABOUT THE INCIDENT.

SHE CAME TO QUINCY THE FOLLOWING WEEK. A REPORT AIRED LATER THAT DAY.

STUDENT ASSAULTED

CALLS SOON STARTED COMING IN FROM REPORTERS AND OTHER MEDIA PEOPLE.

MOST OF THE NEWSPAPER REPORTS WENT OUT OF THEIR WAY TO POINT OUT THAT REGGIE WAS AN HONOR ROLL STUDENT. THE IMPLICATION SEEMED TO BE THAT IF HE'D HAD POOR GRADES OR WAS A DROPOUT, THE COPS' ATTACK WOULD HAVE BEEN MORE JUSTIFIED.

WHAT IF IT HAD HAPPENED TO A STUDENT WHO WAS IN A GANG? WOULD ANYONE HAVE CARED THEN?

SOON AFTER THE NEWS REPORTS, WE RECEIVED A CALL FROM THE OFFICE OF PROFESSIONAL STANDARDS, WHO WERE NOW ANXIOUS TO BEGIN AN INVESTIGATION. THE STUDENTS COULDN'T BE INTERVIEWED WITHOUT PARENTAL CONSENT, AN ARRANGEMENT THAT ALLOWED US A DAY TO PREP THE KIDS.

TELL THEM EVERYTHING YOU KNOW ABOUT WHAT HAPPENED, AND ANSWER EVERY QUESTION TRUTHFULLY.

WE DIDN'T HAVE MUCH FAITH IN THE INVESTIGATION. STATISTICS SHOWED THAT ONLY 10% OF COMPLAINTS RESULTED IN DISCIPLINARY ACTION AGAINST THE ACCUSED OFFICER.

THE INTERVIEWS WERE TENSE, SOLEMN AFFAIRS. I WAS ALLOWED TO SIT IN, BUT HAD TO REMAIN SILENT.

JUST TELL THE TRUTH...

AT QUINCY, WE WERE BECOMING CONCERNED THAT THE CASE MIGHT NOT BE RESOLVED BY THE END OF THE SCHOOL YEAR.

WE DECIDED TO CIRCULATE PETITIONS DIRECTED AT MAYOR DALEY AND STATE'S ATTORNEY O'MALLEY. 9 PAGES OF SIGNATURES WERE COLLECTED.

FORTY STUDENTS GATHERED TO DELIVER THE PETITIONS DOWNTOWN. ALTHOUGH NEITHER THE MAYOR NOR THE STATE'S ATTORNEY MET WITH THEM, THE STUDENTS MADE THEIR VOICES HEARD.

I'M ALMA NAVARRO, A STUDENT AT QUINCY SCHOOL. IT BRINGS TEARS TO MY EYES THAT THE INJUSTICES CAUSED BY 2 OF OUR CHICAGO POLICE OFFICERS ARE GOING UNPUNISHED.

EVERY KID WHO SPOKE CAME BACK TO THE THEME OF JUSTICE. WHAT DID IT MEAN FOR THEM? HOW LONG WOULD THEY BELIEVE IT?

TWO WEEKS LATER, AS REGGIE AND HIS CLASSMATES FILLED QUINCY'S GYM ON GRADUATION DAY, I WAS LEFT WONDERING IF OUR EFFORTS HAD BEEN IN VAIN.

WHAT MESSAGE HAD I SENT TO REGGIE AND THE KIDS? HAD THEY LEARNED ABOUT FIGHTING INJUSTICE AND SPEAKING WITH A COLLECTIVE VOICE?

OR HAD THEY JUST BEEN MADE TO FEEL POWERLESS?

REGGIE WILSON.

CLAP CLAP WOOHOO! CLAP CLAP CLAP YEAH, REGGIE! CLAP CLAP

THE KIDS' CHEERS WERE NOT OF VICTORY, BUT AN ACKNOWLEDGEMENT OF THE STRUGGLE ITSELF, OF THE COURAGE REGGIE AND THE WITNESSES HAD SHOWN IN TAKING A BRAVE STAND AGAINST THE POLICE.

IT WAS A MOVING SHOW OF UNITY FOR A KID WHO THE REST OF THE STUDENTS NOW SAW AS ONE OF THEIR OWN.

IT WAS NOT UNTIL THE FOLLOWING FEBRUARY THAT THIS ORDEAL FINALLY REACHED SOME CLOSURE.

NO CHARGES WERE FILED AGAINST EITHER OFFICER, ALLEGEDLY BECAUSE THERE WAS NOT ENOUGH EVIDENCE.

THE OFFICE OF PROFESSIONAL STANDARDS RECOMMENDED DISCIPLINARY ACTION AGAINST "THE BULL," WHO WAS SUSPENDED FOR 30 DAYS WITHOUT PAY.

HIS PARTNER WAS EXONERATED AND LATER PROMOTED TO DETECTIVE.

THE CIVIL SUIT WAS SETTLED OUT OF COURT. THE CITY PAID REGGIE $60,000 IN DAMAGES. $20,000 WENT TO ATTORNEY FEES.

EW&F SOLD OUT!

AROUND THE SAME TIME, I HEARD THAT EARTH, WIND & FIRE WERE EMBARKING ON A REUNION TOUR.

AS YOU GLIDE IN YOUR STRIDE WITH THE WIND AS YOU FLY AWAY BRING A SMILE TO YOUR LIPS AND SAY I AM FREE, YES I'M FREE NOW I'M ON MY WAY.

REGGIE

WHAT I LEARNED IN CHURCH IS THAT YOU SUPPOSED TO TREAT PEOPLE THE WAY YOU WANT TO BE TREATED. TREAT YOUR NEIGHBOR AS YOURSELF.

WE GOTTA BE KIND TO ONE ANOTHER.

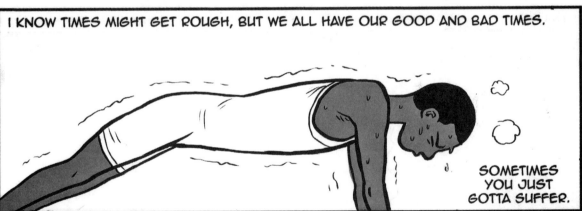

I KNOW TIMES MIGHT GET ROUGH, BUT WE ALL HAVE OUR GOOD AND BAD TIMES.

SOMETIMES YOU JUST GOTTA SUFFER.

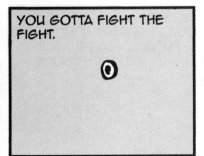

YOU GOTTA FIGHT THE FIGHT.

KEEP GOING.

KEEP PUSHING YOURSELF.

ONE OF MY BIGGEST STRUGGLES IS TRYING TO MAKE GOOD GRADES. IT'S REAL TOUGH. I TRY TO PAY ATTENTION, BUT MY MIND ALWAYS WANDER OFF AND STUFF.

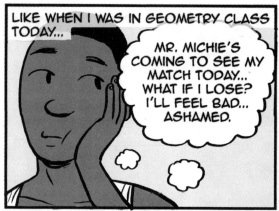

LIKE WHEN I WAS IN GEOMETRY CLASS TODAY...

MR. MICHIE'S COMING TO SEE MY MATCH TODAY... WHAT IF I LOSE? I'LL FEEL BAD... ASHAMED.

THE TEACHER WAS LIKE...

SEE WHAT I'M TALKING ABOUT? YOU'RE ALWAYS DAYDREAMING.

THAT'S WHY YOU DON'T NEVER GET NO GOOD GRADES IN HERE.

I WANT RESPECT. I WANT TO BE MORE POPULAR. BUT I'M NOT POPULAR. I'M QUIET. I USUALLY HANG BY MYSELF.

THAT'S WHY I STARTED WRESTLING. TO GET MORE RESPECT FOR MYSELF.

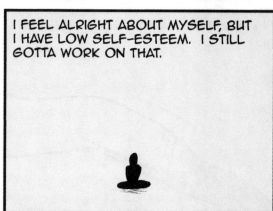

I FEEL ALRIGHT ABOUT MYSELF, BUT I HAVE LOW SELF-ESTEEM. I STILL GOTTA WORK ON THAT.

I FILLED OUT A SURVEY WITH MY MOM'S BOYFRIEND--HE'S TAKING A CLASS AT CHICAGO STATE.

Do you feel good about yourself?

Do you feel down?

Do you feel like a loser?

Do you feel like you're not wanted?

I CAN'T REALLY SEE ANY GOOD QUALITIES THAT I HAVE RIGHT NOW. MAYBE IN THE FUTURE, I'LL BE ABLE TO SEE THEM, BUT NOT RIGHT NOW.

WHEN I SEE POLICE, I STILL THINK ABOUT IT...

I KNOW THERE'S SOME DIRTY COPS OUT THERE. THERE'S SOME WHITE PEOPLE OUT THERE WHO ARE RACISTS, WHO DON'T LIKE BLACKS.

I DIDN'T HATE THE COP WHO DID IT. I JUST THOUGHT WHAT HE DID TO ME WASN'T RIGHT.

I HOPE HE CHANGED, AND REALIZED WHAT HE DID WAS WRONG. BUT I CAN'T SAY I FORGIVE HIM, 'CAUSE HE NEVER CAME UP TO ME AND SAID HE WAS SORRY.

THERE'S BEEN MANY PEOPLE WHO HAVE BEEN BRUTALIZED WORSE THAN I WAS, AND THE PEOPLE WHO ATTACKED THEM WERE NEVER BROUGHT TO JUSTICE.

I THINK THE REASON SOMETHING HAPPENED IN MY CASE WAS BECAUSE I HAD A LOT OF WITNESSES.

IF MS. MACIAS WOULDN'T HAVE BEEN THERE, THEY PROBABLY WOULD HAVE THOUGHT WE WERE LYING. ADULTS THINK KIDS BE LYING ALL THE TIME.

IT'S NOT JUST POLICE WHO ARE RACIST. THE WHOLE SYSTEM IS.

MY HISTORY TEACHER SAYS THEY KILLED MARTIN LUTHER KING BECAUSE HE WAS GOING FOR LAWS AT FIRST, BUT AT THE END HE WAS GOING FOR ECONOMICS.

HE REALIZED THAT A LOT OF THE PROBLEMS WERE RELATED TO ECONOMIC THEORY. THE OLDER HE GOT, THE SMARTER HE GOT, AND THE MORE HE REALIZED WHAT NEEDED TO BE DONE.

THE BLACK PANTHER PARTY KNEW IT, TOO--THAT IT WAS ALL ABOUT ECONOMICS. THAT WE NEEDED BETTER HOUSING, BETTER SCHOOLS, BETTER JOBS, BETTER EDUCATION...

AND IT'S STILL HAPPENING. IT'S STILL GOING ON.

To Be Continued

IT WAS ABOUT 9:40 ON THE MORNING OF QUINCY'S 8TH GRADE GRADUATION.

I'D BEEN UP UNTIL 4 A.M. EDITING A VIDEO FOR THE CEREMONY, AND ARRIVED AT SCHOOL JUST AFTER 7 TO HELP SET UP.

AS I MADE ANOTHER ATTEMPT TO KNOT MY TIE, I COULD HEAR THE STUDENTS LINING UP IN THE HALL.

I STEPPED OUT INTO A SEA OF BLUE ROBES, HUGGED KIDS, SHOOK HANDS...

ILLUSTRATED BY STEPHANY JIMENEZ

I SPUN AROUND TO SEE YESENIA PEREZ. EVEN WITH THE SLIGHTLY OVERDONE MAKEUP, SHE LOOKED BETTER.

BETTER, THAT IS, THAN SHE HAD 2 WEEKS EARLIER...

YESENIA?

NEED TO TALK?

UH-HUH...

COME ON.

IS SOMETHING GOING ON AT HOME?

NOTHING NEW.

HAS YOUR DAD COME AROUND LATELY?

NO, IT'S NOT THAT.

WHAT IS IT THEN? SOMETHING'S BOTHERING YOU.

I DON'T WANT TO LEAVE. I DON'T WANT THIS YEAR TO BE OVER.

YESENIA HAD BEEN AT QUINCY SINCE KINDERGARTEN. NINE OF THE 14 YEARS OF HER LIFE HAD BEEN SPENT THERE.

I CAN'T MAKE IT IN HIGH SCHOOL! SOMETHING BAD'S GOING TO HAPPEN! I CAN FEEL IT!

DON'T SAY THAT. YOU'RE GOING TO BE OK. YOU KNOW WHY?

BECAUSE YOU'RE STRONG.

I'M NOT...

YES, YOU ARE.

A LOT OF THINGS COULD HAVE STOPPED YOU. YOU HAVEN'T JUST MADE IT, YOU'VE DONE WELL. THERE'S NO REASON YOU CAN'T DO THAT IN HIGH SCHOOL AND COLLEGE AND WHEREVER ELSE YOU WANT TO GO.

I'M NOT GOING TO SAY IT ISN'T GOING TO BE HARD, BUT, YESENIA, YOU CAN MAKE IT. I BELIEVE IT. I BELIEVE IN YOU.

KARINA LOPEZ HAD BEEN YESENIA'S BEST FRIEND SINCE 5TH GRADE.

IS SHE OK?

YEAH, JUST A LITTLE SCARED.

WE DIDN'T KNOW WHERE YOU WENT. I WAS WORRIED.

I DON'T WANT TO GRADUATE.

THAT'S ALL THAT NEEDED TO BE SAID FOR KARINA TO UNDERSTAND COMPLETELY. SHE HAD FELT THE SAME ANXIETY.

TWO WEEKS LATER, THE MEMORY OF THAT MOMENT WAS STILL STRONG AS YESENIA STOOD PROUDLY BEFORE ME.

ARE YOU READY?

WELL, I BETTER BE. IT'S GONNA HAPPEN WHETHER I'M READY OR NOT.

8TH GRADE GRADUATIONS ARE MAJOR EVENTS IN THE PUBLIC SCHOOLS OF CHICAGO.

PARENTS OF ALL SHAPES, SIZES, AND DEMEANORS--SOME WHO HAVE DILIGENTLY SUPPORTED THEIR CHILDREN, OTHERS WHO ARE WALKING INTO THE SCHOOL FOR THE FIRST TIME IN YEARS--ALL DUTIFULLY WHOOP IT UP WHEN THEIR KID'S NAME IS CALLED. IT'S A BIG DEAL.

THE REASON FOR ALL THIS HOOPLA, ACCORDING TO CYNICAL CHICAGOANS, IS THAT "IT'S THE ONLY GRADUATION MOST OF THESE KIDS WILL EVER HAVE." IT'S A HARSH SENTIMENT, BUT STATISTICS BEAR OUT ITS PESSIMISM.

STATS DON'T LIE.

↑40% Chicago High School Student Dropout

Reasons:
✓ early pregnancies
✓ unsafe turfs
✓ money worries
✓ splintered families
✓ gangs

NO ONE UNDERSTANDS THIS BETTER THAN PARENTS IN NEIGHBORHOOD'S LIKE QUINCY'S.

LIKE THE FATHER WHO WORKS 2 JOBS, MAYBE 3...

AND STILL MOST FIND THE TIME TO REPAIR THE LEAKY FAUCET THE LAND-LORD REFUSES TO FIX.

THE MOTHER WHO SPENDS 2ND SHIFT HOURS IN A FACTORY...

AND FIRST SHIFT HOURS LEARNING ENGLISH...

¿COMO ESTA USTED?

HOW ARE YOU?

WHO STILL MUST COME HOME TO PREPARE TAQUITOS AND SCRUB CLOTHES.

THE SINGLE PARENT WHO SENSES THAT THE DECK OF TECHNOLOGICAL "PROGRESS" IS BEING INCREASINGLY STACKED AGAINST HER.

WHO, ARMED WITH HER HARD-WON HIGH SCHOOL DIPLOMA, CAN ONLY FIND MINIMUM-WAGE, NO-BENEFIT JOBS.

WHO HAS EVERY REASON TO GIVE UP ON HERSELF AND HER KIDS, BUT DOESN'T.

THESE PARENTS REJOICE AT ELEMENTARY SCHOOL GRADUATIONS NOT BECAUSE THEY ARE WITNESSING A LAST HURRAH, BUT BECAUSE A DAY THEY HAVE WORKED FOR, SACRIFICED FOR, HOPED AND PRAYED FOR HAS ARRIVED AT LAST.

AT 10 AM, THE 8TH GRADE GRADUATES BEGAN FILING INTO THE GYM.

BOB... ANY SIGN OF THE MARIACHI BAND?

NOT YET.

THEY SHOULD BE HERE BY NOW...

WHAT IF THEY DON'T SHOW UP?

IT'S A SURPRISE, SO NO ONE WILL KNOW TO BE DISAPPOINTED.

IF THEY DON'T SHOW UP, YOU AND ME ARE GOING UP THERE AND SINGING OURSELVES.

AS I WATCHED THE GRADUATES ASSEMBLE, I WONDERED:

WHAT HAVE I REALLY TAUGHT THESE KIDS?

WHAT HAVE THEY GOTTEN OUT OF OUR TIME TOGETHER? HAVE THEY BECOME MORE CONFIDENT? MORE COMPASSIONATE?

MORE LITERATE? MORE LIKELY TO QUESTION THE WORLD AROUND THEM?

WHAT CONNECTED WITH THEM, WHAT PUSHED THEM TO THINK OR ACT? WHAT MATTERED?

WHAT HAD MATTERED FOR MARTIN RUIZ WERE 2 40-MINUTE-LONG MULTIPLE CHOICE TESTS BACK IN APRIL.

A NEW BOARD OF EDUCATION POLICY MANDATED THAT IN ORDER TO GRADUATE, 8TH GRADERS HAD TO MEET BENCHMARKS ON THE READING AND MATH PORTIONS. MARTIN HAD EASILY MADE THE CUT ON THE MATH PORTION, BUT HE BARELY MISSED IT IN READING WITH A SCORE OF 6.8.

Hang in there

MARTIN HAD WORKED HARD ALL YEAR, GOTTEN DECENT GRADES, AND HIS TEACHERS AGREED THAT HE WAS READY TO MOVE ON. BUT NONE OF THAT MADE ANY DIFFERENCE. 6.9 WAS THE LOWEST PASSING SCORE, AND NOTHING ELSE MATTERED.

I THOUGHT OF GLORIA ROMERO, THE SALUTATORIAN MY FIRST YEAR AT QUINCY.

SHE WAS A DILIGENT STUDENT, STUDENT COUNCIL VICE-PRESIDENT, AN ACTIVE PARTICIPANT IN AFTERSCHOOL PROGRAMS...

AT THE AGE OF 15, GLORIA WAS PREGNANT AND NO LONGER ATTENDING SCHOOL.

I KNEW THE BIRTH OF A BABY WOULDN'T STOP HER FROM GOING AFTER HER DREAMS. BUT I ALSO REALIZED HOW MUCH MORE DIFFICULT IT MADE FINISHING HER EDUCATION.

IT WAS HARD TO IMAGINE A MORE TREACHEROUS PATH THAN THE ONE THAT BROUGHT RAMON TORRES TO HIS SEAT.

THE ONLY CERTAINTY IN RAMON'S LIFE HAD BEEN A PERPETUAL UNCERTAINTY, A DOMESTIC REVOLVING DOOR OF DISILLUSIONMENT AND BROKEN PROMISES. FOR YEARS, HE'D BOUNCED AROUND FROM ONE HOME TO ANOTHER, STAYING WITH FRIENDS, COUSINS, IN GARAGES...

Ramon's stuff

AS I WATCHED HIM AWAIT HIS DIPLOMA, I FOUND MYSELF IN AWE OF HIS IRREPRESSIBLE WILL.

IT'S 11:45. WHERE ARE THE MARIACHIS?

I NOTICED ELENA SANTOS ACROSS THE GYM.

AS I WATCHED HER, I WONDERED IF THE SAME MEMORY THAT WAS GNAWING AT ME WAS TROUBLING HER.

A FEW WEEKS EARLIER, ELENA HAD BEEN THE DOMINANT VOICE IN A VIDEOTAPED STUDENT DISCUSSION ABOUT THE PRESENCE OF VIOLENCE IN THEIR LIVES.

DO YOU BELIEVE THE STATEMENT THAT ONE PERSON CAN MAKE A DIFFERENCE?

ONE PERSON CAN MAKE A DIFFERENCE, BUT YOU NEED MORE PEOPLE TO REALLY CHANGE SOMETHING.

OUTSIDE THE WINDOW I SAW VIC TRUJILLO, WHO HAD BEEN AN 8TH GRADER AT QUINCY THE YEAR BEFORE.

ON THE OTHER SIDE OF THE BUILDING, A FUN DAY WAS UNDER WAY FOR THE SCHOOL'S KINDERGARTNERS.

THE GAMES STOPPED BRIEFLY AT THE SOUND OF GUNFIRE, BUT RESUMED JUST AS QUICKLY.

ALL THESE THOUGHTS COMPETED IN MY HEAD AS I WATCHED ELENA. I DIDN'T KNOW WHAT TO FEEL.

SHE WAS BRIGHT, SENSITIVE, AT THE START OF HER LIFE, BUT WITH ONLY THE MOST FRAGILE HOPE FOR HERSELF OR HER WORLD.

COULD I BLAME HER? COULD I BE HOPEFUL FOR HER?

IN MOVIES AND TV SHOWS ABOUT SCHOOL, THE GRADUATION SCENE IS THE FAMILIAR CLOSER.

BUT REAL LIVES DON'T END WITH CAPS BEING TOSSED IN THE AIR IN SLOW MOTION.

SOME OF THESE KIDS WOULD COMPLETELY DISAPPEAR FROM MY LIFE AFTER TODAY.

OTHERS I MIGHT ONLY RUN INTO AT THE GROCERY STORE OR WAVE TO AS THEY STOOD AT A BUS STOP.

BUT A HANDFUL WOULD CONTINUE TO SEEK OUT MY GUIDANCE, AND WITH A FEW I MIGHT DEVELOP SOME SORT OF LASTING TIE. A FRIENDSHIP.

SLOWLY, THE GRADUATES BEGAN TO FILE PAST ME TOWARDS THE EXITS. ACROSS THE GYM, I CAUGHT A GLIMPSE OF YESENIA.

RAMON REVELED IN THE MOMENT EVEN THOUGH NO ONE IN HIS FAMILY HAD SHOWN UP.

ELENA MOVED SLOWLY AT THE END OF THE LINE. I WAVED TO HER, BUT IN ALL THE COMMOTION, SHE DIDN'T NOTICE.

SHE WAS ON HER WAY NOW, READY OR NOT.

Yesenia

WHEN I WAS REAL LITTLE, I WAS SCARED OF SCHOOL.

MY MOM ALWAYS MAKES FUN OF ME. SHE SAYS I'M A PRESCHOOL DROPOUT.

IT'S 'CAUSE I WAS A VERY NERVOUS CHILD. IF ANYBODY SCREAMED AT ME, I WOULD GET SCARED.

WELL, MY PRESCHOOL TEACHER WOULD SCREAM A LOT, AND... I WOULD GET REAL SCARED AND THROW UP.

FOR REAL, I WOULD THROW UP! SO MY MOM HAD TO PICK ME UP EVERY DAY. AFTER A WHILE, SHE JUST STOPPED TAKING ME.

I THINK A LOT MORE TEACHERS SHOULD TAKE THE TIME OUT TO SEE THE POTENTIAL KIDS REALLY HAVE, INSTEAD OF JUST THE GRADES THEY MAKE.

FOR SOME TEACHERS, IT'S ALL ABOUT GRADES. WHAT YOU GET ON THE PAPER, THAT'S YOU.

TEACHERS SHOULD BE ENCOURAGING STUDENTS, TELLING THEM

YOU HAVE THIS GIFT. YOU'RE VERY GOOD AT THIS.

THEN KIDS MIGHT SEE SCHOOL IN A DIFFERENT WAY. MOST KIDS, IF YOU SAY THE WORD SCHOOL, THEY SAY

UUGH!

BUT THEY SHOULD SEE IT LIKE, I CAN LEARN, I CAN BE SOMEONE, I CAN GET SMARTER.

MY MOM GOT A DEGREE FROM A 2-YEAR COLLEGE FOR EARLY CHILDHOOD EDUCATION, BUT SHE'S NOT WORKING IN THAT FIELD. SHE HAD A JOB AT A DAYCARE CENTER, BUT THEY WERE PAYING HER MINIMUM WAGE.

THEY PAY HER MORE IN THE FACTORY, WHERE SHE DOESN'T EVEN NEED A COLLEGE DEGREE.

I WORRY ABOUT THAT SOMETIMES. LIKE AM I GOING TO SPEND 4 YEARS IN COLLEGE AND STILL NOT BE ABLE TO GET A GOOD JOB?

WHEN I WAS YOUNGER, MY DAD, HE USED TO HIT US ALL THE TIME. BEFORE WE WERE BORN, HE HIT MY MOM.

ONE SATURDAY, IT WAS JUST US, THE KIDS, RIGHT? WE SAW THE POLICE CAR OUTSIDE AND WE WERE ALL SCARED TO ANSWER THE DOOR.

THEY CAME IN WITH MY MOM AND SHE TOLD US THEY HAD ARRESTED OUR DAD 'CAUSE HE HAD HIT HER IN THE CURRENCY EXCHANGE.

THAT'S WHY MY MOTHER MEANS SO MUCH TO ME. I CONSIDER HER MY MOM AND MY DAD.

I ALWAYS SAY THAT I DON'T HAVE A REAL DAD, 'CAUSE HE NEVER REALLY SHOWED LOVE TOWARD ME.

AND THAT'S WHY I LOOKED UP TO MY MA, BECAUSE SHE GIVES ME HOPE THAT I DON'T NEED ANYBODY.

I DON'T NEED TO DEPEND ON A GUY OR A HUSBAND TO MAKE IT, BECAUSE MY MA MADE IT ON HER OWN.

SHE HAS ALL THIS STRENGTH IN HER, AND ALL THIS COURAGE, AND EVEN AFTER MY DAD LEFT, SHE KEPT PUSHING, YOU KNOW?

THAT'S THE THING I THINK COULD AFFECT MY LIFE MAJORLY. IF SOMETHING HAPPENED TO HER, THAT'S HOW MY LIFE COULD FALL APART.

I LIVE IN AN AREA WITH A GANG RIGHT HERE, AND THERE'S DRUG DEALERS, BUT IT'S NOT LIKE PEOPLE THINK.

I SEE A LOT OF THE YOUNGER KIDS GETTING INVOLVED WITH THE CHURCH: I SEE KIDS TRYING TO TURN THEIR LIVES AROUND.

IT'S NOT LIKE YOU GOTTA GO OUT THERE WITH A GUN AND A BULLETPROOF VEST. PEOPLE HAVE A LOT OF STEROTYPES ABOUT LIVING IN THE CITY.

THEY THINK IT'S ALL DANGEROUS, THAT YOU CAN'T EVEN GO OUT OF YOUR HOUSE, AND IT'S NOT LIKE THAT.

BUT THERE'S PROBLEMS, AND I WANT TO TRY TO MAKE IT BETTER, TO DO SOMETHING TO HELP.

I DON'T WANT TO BE JUST AN AVERAGE PERSON. I WANT TO STAND OUT. I WANT TO BE ABLE TO SAY THAT I ACTUALLY MADE A DIFFERENCE.

AFTERWORD

"SO, WHAT'S THE POINT?"

Have a good summer!

IT'S A QUESTION I GET ASKED OFTEN BY 7TH AND 8TH GRADERS. IF WE ARE READING A POEM THAT THEY DEEM TOO ABSTRACT, OR A DISCUSSION GETS BOGGED DOWN OR OFF TRACK... "WHAT'S THE POINT, MR. MICHIE?"

I'M REMINDED OF THAT QUESTION BY ONE OF THE CRITICISMS I'VE RECEIVED ABOUT *HOLLER*: THAT IT'S NOT CLEAR WHAT I WANT READERS TO COME AWAY WITH.

GRADUATE COHORT LECTURE SERIES

THE STORIES ARE ENGAGING, BUT... WHAT'S YOUR THEORETICAL FRAMEWORK?

I GUESS IT SHOULDN'T BE SURPRISING. THIS IS A COLLECTION OF NARRATIVES, AFTER ALL, NOT A POSITION PAPER. BUT I DIDN'T SELECT THE STORIES AT RANDOM. I HOPED THEY WOULD ADD UP TO A COLLECTIVE ARGUMENT FOR SOME OF THE THINGS I'VE COME TO UNDERSTAND AND BELIEVE ABOUT TEACHING--ESPECIALLY IN POOR OR MARGINALIZED COMMUNITIES.

EDUCATION IS NOT THE FILLING OF A PAIL...

BUT THE LIGHTING OF A FIRE

A BIG PART OF WHAT I WANTED TO CONVEY IS THAT TEACHERS NEED TO SEE THEIR STUDENTS--AS WELL AS THEIR STUDENTS' FAMILIES AND COMMUNITIES--AS FULLY AS POSSIBLE, RECOGNIZING THEIR ASSETS RATHER THAN ZEROING IN ON DEFICITS.

THE BACK OF THE YARDS THE MEDIA NEVER SHOWS

MOST KIDS CAN SNIFF OUT DISRESPECT OR CONDESCENSION A MILE AWAY, AND IF YOU'RE VIEWING THEM OR THEIR COMMUNITY AS FUNDAMENTALLY DEFICIENT, THEY'RE GOING TO PICK UP ON IT.

SWEEPING JUDGMENTS OR ASSUMPTIONS GET YOU NOWHERE IF YOUR GOAL IS TO BE A BETTER TEACHER TO THE KIDS WHO WALK THROUGH YOUR DOOR EACH DAY.

FOR WHITE TEACHERS LIKE ME, IT'S ALSO CRUCIAL TO RECKON WITH OUR OWN RACIAL, CULTURAL, GENDER, AND CLASS IDENTITIES.

BLACK LIVES MATTER

I NEED TO DO AS MUCH AS I CAN TO TRY TO UNDERSTAND THE OBSTACLES MY STUDENTS AND THEIR FAMILIES FACE-- AND BE ON THEIR SIDE.

IMMIGRANTS MAKE AMERICA GREAT

BLACK LIVES MATTER

THE MOST IMPORTANT LESSON, THOUGH, IS THAT THIS IS AN ONGOING COMMITMENT. THIRTY YEARS AFTER STARTING OUT AS A TEACHER, I'M STILL GETTING SCHOOLED.

GOOD TEACHING ALSO REQUIRES LOOKING CRITICALLY AT THE WAY THINGS ARE IN SCHOOLS, QUESTIONING HOW THEY MIGHT BE DIFFERENT, AND TAKING ACTION WHEN THE SITUATION CALLS FOR IT.

Summer!

FOR MOST TEACHERS THIS MEANS STARTING WITH ONE'S OWN CLASSROOM: CAN STUDENTS SEE THEMSELVES AND THEIR EXPERIENCES REFLECTED IN THE CURRICULUM?

UNDOCUMENTED UNAFRAID
NO TENEMOS MIEDO

ARE THEIR VOICES BEING HEARD, THEIR OPINIONS BEING VALUED, THEIR CREATIVE ENERGIES BEING TAPPED?

FOR OUR DOCUMENTARY, WE INTERVIEWED UNDOCUMENTED STUDENTS...

BUT IT ALSO MEANS LOOKING AT BROADER PRACTICES AND POLICIES, AND ASKING QUESTIONS ABOUT WHO THEY HARM AND WHOSE INTERESTS THEY SERVE.

YES, GOOD TEACHERS CAN, AND DO, MAKE A TREMENDOUS DIFFERENCE. GOOD SCHOOLS ARE ESSENTIAL IN EVERY NEIGHBORHOOD. BUT TEACHERS AND SCHOOLS ALONE CAN'T UNDO THE INEQUITIES AND INJUSTICES THAT TOO MANY KIDS IN NEIGHBORHOODS LIKE QUINCY'S FACE.

XENOPHOBIA, RACISM, POVERTY, SEGREGATION, POLICE VIOLENCE, INEQUITABLE FUNDING. WITHOUT ALSO FACING DOWN THESE ILLS, WHICH LAND DISPROPORTIONATELY ON BLACK AND BROWN FAMILIES AND THEIR CHILDREN, PUBLIC SCHOOLS IN THIS COUNTRY WILL STRUGGLE TO FULFILL THEIR PROMISE.

JUST AS I DID IN MY EARLY YEARS, I STILL TRY TO KEEP ONE EYE ON THE BIGGER PICTURE AND THE OTHER ON THE KIDS IN FRONT OF ME.

WHAT'S UP, MR. MICHIE?

HEY, JALISSA!

THE YOUNG PEOPLE THAT I TEACH IN BACK OF THE YARDS ARE FULL OF PROMISE AND POSSIBILITY. THEY ARE BRIGHT, BEAUTIFUL, FRAGILE, FLAWED, COURAGEOUS, AND INCREDIBLY RESILIENT YOUNG PEOPLE. THEY HAVE A LOT TO SAY.

HOLLER IF YOU HEAR.

ABOUT THE ARTISTS/AUTHORS

AUGUST ABITANG LIKES TO CREATE THINGS.

RYAN ALEXANDER-TANNER IS A CARTOONIST AND EDUCATOR. HE HAS CREATED COMICS FOR A LONG LIST OF CLIENTS AND COLLABORATORS THAT INCLUDE THE NIB, PLANNED PARENTHOOD, AND *THE NEW YORK TIMES*. THIS IS HIS SECOND BOOK FOR TEACHERS COLLEGE PRESS, THE FIRST BEING *TO TEACH: THE JOURNEY, IN COMICS* (WITH WILLIAM AYERS). WWW.OHYESVERYNICE.COM

ISABELLE DIZON IS A 17-YEAR-OLD SENIOR AT LINDBLOM MATH AND SCIENCE ACADEMY IN CHICAGO. DRIVEN BY CARTOON STORYTELLING AND HER CULTURE, ISABELLE CHOSE TO ILLUSTRATE NANCY'S STORY.

DALIN DOHRN WAS BORN IN NEW YORK AND NOW LIVES IN CHICAGO WITH HER FAMILY AND TWO EXCEPTIONALLY STUPID CATS. *HOLLER IF YOU HEAR ME* IS HER FIRST GRAPHIC NOVEL.

SARITA HERNÁNDEZ IS AN ARTS EDUCATOR, ORAL HXSTORIAN, AND PRINT/ZINEMAKER FROM CALIFAS. SARITA IS CO-FOUNDER OF MARIMACHA MONARCA PRESS, A QUEER AND TRANS* ARTISTS OF COLOR COLLECTIVE BASED ON CHICAGO'S SOUTH SIDE.

TATUM HOWLETT IS AN INTERDISCIPLINARY ARTIST FROM THE PACIFIC NORTHWEST. SHE LIKES LOUD MUSIC, HORROR MOVIES, AND CHOPPING FIREWOOD. MORE OF HER WORK CAN BE FOUND ON HER INSTAGRAM, @DEEPFRIEDGUTS.

STEPHANY JIMENEZ IS A CHICAGO PUBLIC SCHOOL ART TEACHER IN THE BACK OF THE YARDS NEIGHBORHOOD. SHE WAS BORN AND RAISED ON THE SOUTH SIDE OF CHICAGO LIKE MOST OF HER STUDENTS, AND HOPES TO MAKE A PROFOUND IMPACT ON THEIR LIVES AS HER TEACHERS DID FOR HER.

XENA LOPEZ IS A SELF-TAUGHT ARTIST BASED IN CHICAGO. WHILST PURSUING A DEGREE IN THE FINE ARTS AND BIOLOGY, SHE ALSO SERVES AS THE PRESIDENT OF THE ARTISTS ASSOCIATION AT NORTHEASTERN ILLINOIS UNIVERSITY.

GREGORY MICHIE HAS BEEN AN EDUCATOR IN CHICAGO FOR NEARLY 30 YEARS. IN ADDITION TO TEACHING, HE ENJOYS EXPLORING MEXICO, SEEING MOVIES ON THE BIG SCREEN, AND LISTENING TO 1970S AND 80S FUNK. FIND HIM ON TWITTER @GREGORYMICHIE.

HENNESSY MORALES IS CURRENTLY A 15-YEAR-OLD SOPHOMORE IN HIGH SCHOOL WHO GREW UP IN URBAN NEIGHBORHOODS. ALONG WITH PERFECT DRAWINGS WITH NO FLAWS (...), THEY ALSO ENJOY PLAYING THE UKULELE, WRITING, READING, AND GENERALLY LIVING LIKE A HERMIT CRAB.

CITLALI PEREZ IS A PROUD HIJA DE PADRES INMIGRANTES. SHE GREW UP IN BACK OF THE YARDS AND COMES FROM A BIG FAMILY OF EIGHT. SHE GRADUATED FROM BACK OF THE YARDS HIGH SCHOOL AND NOW ATTENDS DEPAUL UNIVERSITY THANKS TO HER MENTORS. HER INTEREST IN ART WAS INFLUENCED BY HER DAD, WHO HAD TO GIVE UP DRAWING FOR DEMOLITION. SHE BELIEVES IN THE ABOLITION OF ICE, BORDERS, POLICE, AND PRISONS.

DEON REED IS A MULTIDISCIPLINARY ARTIST BASED IN CHICAGO. HE FOCUSES ON THE DICHOTOMY AND SIMILARITIES OF HUMAN NATURE AND LOGIC. HE STARTED A CREATIVE COLLECTIVE AND IS CURRENTLY WORKING ON THAT.